JOHN DEWEY'S PHILOSOPHY OF SPIRIT, WITH THE 1897 LECTURE ON HEGEL

JOHN DEWEY'S PHILOSOPHY OF SPIRIT, WITH THE 1897 LECTURE ON HEGEL

JOHN R. SHOOK AND JAMES A. GOOD

FORDHAM UNIVERSITY PRESS   NEW YORK   2010

Copyright © 2010 Fordham University Press

All rights reserved. No part of this publication may be reproduced, stored in a retrieval system, or transmitted in any form or by any means—electronic, mechanical, photocopy, recording, or any other—except for brief quotations in printed reviews, without the prior permission of the publisher.

Fordham University Press has no responsibility for the persistence or accuracy of URLs for external or third-party Internet websites referred to in this publication and does not guarantee that any content on such websites is, or will remain, accurate or appropriate.

Fordham University Press also publishes its books in a variety of electronic formats. Some content that appears in print may not be available in electronic books.

Library of Congress Cataloging-in-Publication Data
is available from the publisher.

12 11 10   5 4 3 2 1
First edition

Contents

Preface   vii

Editorial Procedures for Class Lecture Notes
by Center for Dewey Studies   xi

Part I. Dewey's Philosophy of Spirit

Dewey's Naturalized Philosophy of Spirit and Religion   3
  John R. Shook

Rereading Dewey's "Permanent Hegelian Deposit"   56
  James A. Good

Part II. Dewey's 1897 Lecture on Hegel

Hegel's Philosophy of Spirit: 1897, University of Chicago   93
  John Dewey

Notes   177

Index   193

Preface

In a brief autobiographical essay published in 1930, John Dewey acknowledged that Hegel had "left a permanent deposit" in his thought, but he was evasive about the details of Hegel's influence. Dewey's admission fueled a debate, which shows no sign of abating even now, about the extent to which his later works contain a mixture of Hegelian and pragmatist elements. Since the publication of Morton White's *The Origins of Dewey's Instrumentalism* in 1943, Dewey scholars have held that he made a complete break from Hegelianism around the turn of the twentieth century. Scholars have argued about the exact timing of Dewey's conversion, but all agree that it occurred and that it happened sometime during the period 1894–1903. This interpretation, however, never put to rest questions about Hegelian elements in Dewey's mature thought, particularly in *Experience and Nature* (1925), *Art as Experience* (1934), and *A Common Faith* (1934).

John Shook's book *Dewey's Empirical Theory of Knowledge and Reality* (2000) was the first to break with the traditional reading of Dewey's turn from Hegelianism toward pragmatism, arguing instead that Dewey's mature philosophy was a gradual and naturalistic modification of his Hegelianism. For evidence, Shook focused primarily on Dewey's changing relationship to British neo-Hegelian philosophers. James Good's book *A Search for Unity in Diversity: The "Permanent Hegelian Deposit" in the Philosophy of John Dewey* (2005) extended Shook's argument by comparing Dewey's thought to recent readings of Hegel. His primary argument is that scholars have been mistaken about Dewey's Hegelianism because they assume that the neo-Hegelian, metaphysical/

theological reading of Hegel was the only one available to Dewey. When we examine Dewey's Hegelianism in the light of recent humanistic/historicist readings of Hegel, we find a far more significant Hegelian deposit throughout Dewey's oeuvre.

The arguments of both books receive weighty support from one of Dewey's unpublished lectures—"Hegel's Philosophy of Spirit"—for a graduate seminar he taught at the University of Chicago in 1897. In the University of Chicago *Annual Register,* the course was titled "Seminar in the Philosophy of Hegel" and was described in the following way:

> Hegel's Lesser Logic and Philosophy of Mind, as translated by Wallace, will be made the basis of study. Points of connection with the thought of his predecessors, especially Kant and Spinoza, will be studied, and Hegel's own ideas will be further developed by reference to selected portions of the Phenomenology, the Philosophy of Law, and the Aesthetics. For graduate students.[1]

This lecture is no longer extant in Dewey's own hand, but it survives in three nearly identical bound typescripts of one hundred and three pages, titled "Hegel's Philosophy of Spirit." The highly grammatical and readable text suggests that the typist was either a stenographer recording Dewey's spoken lecturing or worked directly from excellent student notes or perhaps Dewey's own notes. Any of these three accounts can explain how nearly identical typescripts (suffering only from occasional dropped letters or an odd gap between words) were produced by typewriter using carbon paper. The lecture published in this volume is the result of the transcription and copyediting of the staff of the Center for Dewey Studies in accord with its editing principles (see "Editorial Procedures for Class Lecture Notes"). The Center for Dewey Studies holds copyright on all unpublished works of John Dewey and has granted permission to publish this lecture.

We cannot pause here to compare in detail this 1897 text with the handwritten lecture notes by Eliza Jane Read Sunderland of Dewey's University of Michigan course in winter 1891, also titled "Hegel's Philosophy of Spirit." This set of notes in the Sunderland Manuscript Collection at Bentley Historical Library is very similar to the 1897 typescripts. The large degree of repetition suggests that Dewey was content to repeat most of his primary views on Hegel during much of the 1890s. Considered together, these two lectures indicate that Dewey was well versed in the details of Hegel's intellectual development, his German context, and his writings and that Dewey was still quite sympathetic to Hegel as late as 1897. The 1897 lecture complements evidence in his published writings to support the view that, during the 1890s, Dewey shifted from neo-Hegelianism to a humanist/historicist reading of Hegel and that the latter interpretation of Hegel left a far more significant deposit in his mature thought than neo-Hegelianism. On this view, Dewey's mature philosophy can be seen to be a non-Marxist and nonmetaphysical type of left Hegelianism.

To further experiment with this stance on Dewey and Hegel, we propose in our chapters to explore Dewey's philosophy of religion in general and his inheritance from Hegel of a "philosophy of spirit" in particular. We agree that Dewey did have a philosophy of spirit, that it was heavily indebted to Hegelian themes, and that Dewey's resulting philosophy of religion is a key component of his social and political theory. Shook's chapter offers an examination of religion's role in Dewey's philosophy throughout his career. Dewey's understanding of the functions of religion and religious experience in morality and society are indebted to Hegelian themes, and so is Dewey's theory of democratic politics and its manner of handling the future of religion. Good gives a detailed explanation of Dewey's presentation of Hegel in the 1897 lecture "Hegel's Philosophy of Spirit." Of special significance for Dewey's maturing thought is his historicist and progressivist view of Hegel's treatment of freedom, religion, morality, and politics. For Dewey, Hegel's philosophy of spirit leads directly to the democratic fellowship of common humanity, which becomes the cornerstone of Dewey's own politics.

We extend special thanks to Larry Hickman, Director of the Center for Dewey Studies at Southern Illinois University, for his cooperation with and encouragement of this project. Our editor at Fordham University Press, Helen Tartar, has also been unfailingly supportive, and her efficient and patient assistance made this book possible.

Editorial Procedures for Class Lecture Notes by Center for Dewey Studies

In general, we are operating on a policy of minimal regularization or interference with the text. Although we are dealing for the most part with lecture notes taken by others of Dewey's lectures, the text is the closest thing we have to Dewey's words. We correct what is clearly wrong (such as typographical errors and incorrect bibliographical information), but make no attempt to standardize the text.

Spelling and punctuation. We allow a wide latitude in these areas. If it is possible to consider the spelling of a word acceptable (particularly for its time), we do not change it. Within a set of lecture notes, we allow alternate spellings (e.g., "esthetic" and "aesthetic," "skepticism" and "scepticism," "insofar" and "in so far"), with possible exceptions where instances of a word are in close proximity. Ampersands are expanded to "and," abbreviations are expanded, and numbers are written in full unless in a listing or outline. Punctuation is changed where necessary for the purpose of clarity. No record is provided of these sorts of changes; where substantive changes are made, however, annotation is provided.

For questionable words, a bracketed, italicized question mark [?] is added. For indeterminable words or letters, [*illeg.*] is added. Foreign words are italicized only if underlined in the original. Non-substantive words (e.g., "to" and "the") are added where necessary without record; when referring to a child, "it" is changed to "he" without record; changes made for purposes of tense or subject-verb agreement are not recorded. The addition of substantive words, however, is accompanied by annotation.

Paragraphing. Where the paragraphs are unusually lengthy and it is possible to determine natural breaks, material has been divided into shorter paragraphs.

Quotations. Material within quotation marks is often a paraphrase, rather than a direct quotation. We verify quotations wherever possible and treat them in a variety of ways, depending on the circumstance:

1. No change is made and no annotation is added.
2. No change is made but annotation is added.
3. A minor change is made to reflect the quotation without annotation.
4. A change is made with annotation.

Purely stylistic matters (such as font size for headings, indentions, and in some cases outline style) are made uniform without record. Since many individual patterns are being brought into a unified whole, we have to an extent standardized the stylistic aspect.

Since we cannot be certain whether markings were made by the original notetaker or later by others, we have not accepted handwritten notes and underlining; we have accepted typed underlining as well as corrections.

JOHN DEWEY'S PHILOSOPHY OF SPIRIT,
WITH THE 1897 LECTURE ON HEGEL

PART ONE

DEWEY'S PHILOSOPHY OF SPIRIT

DEWEY'S NATURALIZED PHILOSOPHY OF SPIRIT AND RELIGION
John R. Shook

John Dewey was born October 20, 1859, in Burlington, Vermont. He received his BA from the University of Vermont in 1879 and his PhD in philosophy from Johns Hopkins University in 1884. From 1884 to 1894, he taught philosophy at the University of Michigan, interrupted by a year at the University of Minnesota in 1888–89. From 1894 to 1904, Dewey was professor and chair of the philosophy, psychology, and pedagogy department at the University of Chicago, and with his wife, Alice, he directed an experimental school of primary education. Dewey joined the philosophy faculty of Columbia University in 1905 and taught there until retiring in 1930.

During his years at Columbia he traveled the world as a philosopher, social and political theorist, and educational consultant. Among his major journeys are his lectures in Japan and China from 1919 to 1921, his visit to Turkey in 1924 to recommend educational policy, and a tour of schools in the USSR in 1928. Nonetheless, Dewey never ignored American social issues. He was outspoken on education, domestic and international politics, and numerous social movements. His passionate advocacy of liberal and progressive democracy helped shape the destiny of America and the world. Among the many concerns that attracted Dewey's strong support were labor and unionization, women's suffrage, civil rights, progressive education, the humanist movement, and world peace.

Dewey made seminal contributions to nearly every field and topic in philosophy and psychology. Besides his role as a primary originator of both functionalist and behaviorist psychology, Dewey was a major influence on several allied movements that shaped twentieth-century thought, including empiricism, humanism, naturalism, contextualism, and process philosophy. Dewey ranks with the greatest thinkers of this or any age on the subjects of pedagogy, philosophy of mind, epistemology, philosophy of science, and social and political theory. His pragmatic approaches to ethics, aesthetics, and religion have also remained influential. During his final years, Dewey continued to promote liberal democratic causes and organizations, and published significant political and philosophical writings. Dewey died June 1, 1952, in New York City. At his death, he was acclaimed for having been America's foremost philosopher and public intellectual for several decades.

Stages in Dewey's Philosophy of Religion

John Dewey's naturalistic and humanistic philosophy was grounded on confidence in scientific methods and faith in religious ideals. Unlike many other twentieth-century atheists, Dewey was not hostile toward religious experience. He did demand that such experience be oriented toward human welfare in this world, rather than the next. As a pragmatist, he required that anything "religious" have positive practical significance for human life. Some pragmatists, William James most prominently, supposed that some beliefs in the divine could reasonably pass this practical test, quite apart from the concern that such belief cannot be reasonable from the scientific perspective. James seemed happy to let belief systems undergo the pragmatic test separately, applauding each and every success. This kind of pragmatism demotes coherence among practical beliefs to a secondary matter. Dewey refused to apply the pragmatic test in such a case-by-case manner, disapproving of a too-generous relativism that only superficially harmonizes science with religion. Dewey was also suspicious of any pragmatism that promised a visionary syncretic unification of religions and sciences. He repeatedly denied that there really is anything real denoted by "religion" and claimed that "religion" permits no sharp definition. Religion, in Dewey's view, has no essence to be discerned by examining religions that have already existed or designed by synthesizing a new religion. Only tenuous strands of partially shared features and functions across "religious" practices permit social scientists or philosophers to empirically gesture toward something provisionally labeled "religion."

Yet instead of eliminating religion or ignoring religious phenomena entirely, Dewey searched for the power of faith to find visionary commitment to moral ideals, rather than blind submission to jealous gods or traditional authorities. Intelligently and responsibly pursuing our ideals is all that Dewey asks, but fulfilling this commitment requires taking nature seriously. Scientific knowledge of the natural world is hardly an obstacle, but actually a necessary factor, for effective action. Religion must not merely compromise with science, but its ideals must translate into practical principles applicable to living in this world. Dewey concluded that any idealistic religion truly serious about making the greatest practical difference to humanity's wellbeing must be naturalistic and therefore atheistic. Dewey's philosophical religion was therefore humanistic naturalism: naturalistic enough to take scientific method seriously while humanistic enough to take faithful idealism seriously.

Four stages in Dewey's attitude toward religion can be distinguished. The positive resolutions of each stage were retained in later stages, resulting in a fair amount of continuity across his philosophical maturation toward atheism. Expositions of Dewey's philosophy have not failed to mention the prominence of Hegelian idealism in his early philosophy. However, only a few scholars have emphasized the positive roles that certain Hegelian themes played in his mature thought, and even fewer have considered how formative influences on the young Dewey might explain why these Hegelian themes first became so convincing.[1] The four stages can be briefly characterized as follows. First, as a young boy, Dewey was raised in a pious Calvinist environment. Second, a teenage Dewey heard contradictory views on morality, freedom, and democracy from Burlington intellectual leaders. Third, while in college, Dewey reconciled these contradictories in a Hegelian social idealism that affirmed progressive democracy over traditional religion. Fourth, as a college professor, Dewey naturalistically affirmed Hegelian views on freedom and morality to ground his atheistic and democratic humanism.

Dewey's earliest religious attitudes were formed in a household dominated by his pious Evangelical mother, Lucinda Dewey. Her constants urgings of personal salvation and moral rectitude upon her three sons, in conformity with her own adult conversion to the Calvinistic teachings of New England Congregationalism, inducted the young Dewey into belief in God and church membership. Unlike his mother, however, he did not have a conversion experience of saving grace and preferred the anti-Calvinistic themes of universalism.[2]

Relief from the oppressive atmosphere of home life came from the intellectual life in his hometown. When Dewey was fourteen, the First Congregational Church introduced a new minister of impeccable credentials. Lewis Orsmond Brastow (1834–1912) was a graduate of Bowdoin College and Bangor Theological Seminary, both recognized centers of orthodoxy. Brastow was a liberal pastor who endorsed universal salvation and rejected Biblical literalism and inerrancy. Brastow's professor at Bangor was the legendary Enoch Pond, disciple of Edwardean Nathaniel Emmons. Pond was one of last true defenders of the New Divinity movement inspired by Jonathan Edwards, and a lingering representative of the almost extinct group of Exercisers.[3] Although Pond would have been appalled at Brastow's later universalism, Brastow did not depart from the orthodox tenet of justification by faith alone, and he kept a safe distance from any Arminian entanglement with free will and justification by works. When Brastow's powerful defenses of universalism finally proved too overwhelming to combat at a distance, the Yale Divinity School respected his heritage and orthodoxy enough to call him to be professor of practical theology and homiletics in 1885. Dewey happily attended the First Congregational Church during his undergraduate years and whenever he was visiting home for some years after. During Brastow's tenure in Burlington (1873–84) Dewey had ample opportunity to absorb Brastow's theology, not merely because Dewey's mother ensured regular attendance, but also because Dewey found Brastow's emerging liberal views a relief from stern Calvinism. Dewey's Christian education during those crucial years of exploration and questioning was guided in part by this independent-minded theologian trained in the Edwardean and New Divinity tradition.[4]

In this second stage of Dewey's evolving stance toward religion, Brastow's conclusions about universal salvation and moral responsibility were highly influential. Universalism should, according to Brastow, bring all people together into communities of mutual support and trust; yet Calvinistic predestination and limited atonement open unbridgeable chasms between people. Edwards was therefore wrong to embrace enthusiasm and sudden conversion. Brastow's portrait of repentance and moral growth is corporate and gradualist: we grow in faith and virtue together as a community over lifetimes. This vision of progressive universalism was far more consistent with real life in upstate Vermont during that era, where respect for town hall democracy and social equality was still widespread. Dewey's later reminiscences about formative influences emphasize these two clashing features of New England life, Puritan Christianity and small-town democracy.[5] Universalism was an obvious way to overcome the dualism between the morally worthy and the damned.

Universalism and democracy appeared to support each other. However, the lingering shadow of Edwards still obscured the needed connection between moral responsibility and democracy. Can democratic freedoms be trusted to enhance the moral responsibility of the people? Antidemocrats from Plato to Aquinas to Hobbes distrusted democratic freedom; neither Calvin nor Edwards was a friend of full and open democracy. The sorts of civil freedoms that democratic people seek are not necessarily the same as, but potentially contrary to, the kinds of moral behaviors that religious people respect. America in the nineteenth century still had to grapple with seventeenth-century skepticism toward democracy. Civil freedom meant chaotic anarchy, whereas moral responsibility meant social order. The only political system most of America's founding fathers could imagine was one that counterbalanced democracy with aristocracy, if not a hereditary aristocracy, at least a natural aristocracy of higher virtue and knowledge. After the Civil War, America was continuing to broaden and deepen democracy, but worries over the experimental risks were not abating. Unless freedom could be disentangled from connotations of individual rebellious unlawfulness, democracy suffered from a lack of confidence. A new understanding of freedom in general, and of democratic freedom in particular, was still needed. How can a democratic people be morally responsible?

If Calvinistic predestination and its denial of free will are undemocratic, could the opposite theory of libertarianism be just what was needed? Eighteenth- and nineteenth-century libertarianism postulated that the will, a faculty or capacity separate from the intellect and emotions, is sufficiently detached from ongoing mental processes that it can make independent and uncaused choices. Brastow was no libertarian and repeated the orthodox criticisms of this postulated free will that Edwards formulated so clearly. Brastow's views on the religious life echo the Exercisers' stance, following Edwards, that the mental faculties are a unity and act together. Religion is not based solely on the intellect, or on emotions, or on the will. "Religion is realized only as 'the unity of the soul revealed in feeling, willing, and knowing,' and that soul in its unity becomes the organ of the revealing activity of God."[6] Dewey evidently knew the standard Edwardean attacks on libertarian free will with close familiarity, and he found them so convincing that he approvingly repeated them in two important writings published in 1894, an article titled "Ego and Cause" and a short book titled *The Study of Ethics*. By that time, Dewey had discovered similar rejections of libertarian free will in Hegel's views on freedom and agency, confirming his position. The mature Dewey found no reason to depart from this stance against libertarianism in such books as *Ethics* (1908) and *Human Nature and Conduct* (1922).[7]

Although Dewey heard Brastow insist on assigning the capacities for freedom and responsibility to the whole person, this thoroughly Edwardean tenet raised more questions than it answered. When considered alongside other Calvinistic principles about morality, the role of ideals in moral conduct became highly problematic. Calvinism portrayed moral ideals as delivered from a perfect God who demands perfection from imperfect creatures unable to attain moral conduct by their own efforts. From the Calvinistic standpoint, individual freedom and moral responsibility are strictly incompatible—an increase in moral responsibility in a society necessarily requires a decrease in deliberate freedom exercised by the people. One shows moral responsibility by surrendering one's will to incomprehensible authority and suspending one's intellect to halt questioning. Yet this partitioned notion of moral responsibility clashes with the Edwardean theory of the unity of the soul. Why must moral responsibility require the surrender of personal integrity? Furthermore, Brastow not only suggested that moral conduct is the result of effort by the entire person, but he went further to claim that the capacity of a person to be morally responsible is highly social in nature. In his late teens, Dewey found himself caught between contradictory precepts about morality and moral responsibility. Are moral ideals fixed and perfect, demanding personal submission and obedience? Alternatively, are moral ideals growing and practical, needing social formulation and approval? The first option leads toward aristocratic theocracy; the second leads toward participatory democracy.

Several of Dewey's professors at the University of Vermont, which he entered at age fifteen, similarly held theological views that emphasized social virtues attainable by all people, and moral ideals consistent with the democratic culture of America. This second stage's affirmation of democratic ideals was not yet consistent with the demanding revelations of an authoritative God. Torn between two masters, the people's common intelligence or God's supreme dictates,

Dewey was aroused to search for a philosophical solution. At Vermont he learned about the tradition of reasoned moral thinking from Plato to Kant, where each person's rational capacities could be sufficient for discovering the moral life. Could reason itself reconcile humanity and God?

Dewey's philosophy professor Henry A. P. Torrey (1837–1902) echoed Brastow's insistence that religion and reason are not only compatible but mutually supportive. Torrey's own philosophy tended toward a mixture of romantic idealism with Scottish intuitionalism. Dewey begin to dimly see, in the romantic idealism of Samuel Taylor Coleridge and the intimidating German idealists studied by Torrey, the possibility that Edwards was also near the truth about idealism. As Dewey recollected years later, James Marsh's edition of Coleridge's *Aids to Reflection*, so influential on pedagogy at the University of Vermont, was another counterbalance to the anti-intellectual aspects of Calvinism. Marsh's edition of Coleridge was, in Dewey's recollection of those days, "our spiritual emancipation in Vermont. Coleridge's idea of the spirit came to us as a real relief, because we could be both liberal and pious; and his *Aids to Reflection* book, especially Marsh's edition, was my first Bible."[8] Marsh's introduction emphasizes the significance of Coleridge's views for the free will controversy then animating New England Protestantism, which were familiar to Dewey. Coleridge, inspired by his reading of German idealists, demanded that the only freedom practically relevant for human life is grounded in the intelligent will.[9] Coleridge defined spirit as the "rational will" that guarantees moral freedom. Marsh and Coleridge, in accord with other intuitionalists, defended the superior metaphysical reality of "spirit" over "nature," arguing that the knowing mind can explain the existence of the natural things known, but natural things can never explain the knowing mind. These idealists were supremely confident that people exercising their own free rationality would arrive at the moral principles of Christianity. While at the University of Vermont, Dewey heard various sources assert an intimate connection between reason and will, and proclaim that the moral life is the intellectual life, and both can be the genuinely religious life. Although

Dewey would soon reject New England intuitionalism as too simplistic, this chorus of voices played a key role in Dewey's own emerging conceptions of freedom, moral responsibility, and religious faith.

Two more stimulating experiences made a significant impact on Dewey's intellectual trajectory during these late teenage years. Dewey studied natural evolution during his junior year at Vermont, and a year later in Oil City, Pennsylvania, he had a religious experience. These events did not strike Dewey as contradictory in import. What impressed him about biological evolution, as portrayed in his textbook by Thomas Henry Huxley, *Lessons in Elementary Physiology*, was its holistic model of life as organic unities. Organisms are composed of interdependent cellular parts that function cooperatively to yield the organism's characteristic traits and abilities.[10] Dewey was not suddenly converted to materialism, but he did accept evolution over divine creation. As for Dewey's religious experience, it did not seem as though God were speaking to him, but he did feel intimately connected with reality. Max Eastman reports Dewey's account in 1941 of the event.

> One evening while he sat reading he had what he calls a "mystic experience." It was an answer to that question which still worried him: whether he really meant business when he prayed. It was not a very dramatic mystic experience. There was no vision, not even a definable emotion—just a supremely blissful feeling that his worries were over. Mystic experiences in general, Dewey explains, are purely emotional and cannot be conveyed in words. But when he tries to convey his in words, it comes out like this: "What the hell are you worrying about, anyway? Something that's here is here, and you can just lie back on it." "I've never had any doubts since then," he adds, "nor any beliefs. To me faith means not worrying." Although his religion has so little affirmative content, and has nothing to do, he is sure, with his philosophy, Dewey likens it to the poetic pantheism of Wordsworth, whom he was reading at that time, and to Walt Whitman's sense of oneness with the universe. "I claim I've got religion," he concludes, "and that I got it that night in Oil City."[11]

Uncertain about his career options, and hesitant to pursue the theological education that typically led to the teaching profession, Dewey continued to read Kant, Hegel, and other philosophers developing diverse kinds of idealisms. Some of these idealisms were designed to defend traditional supernaturalism and an all-powerful God. Other idealisms made no place for a supernatural God among the personal minds that make up reality. The idealisms that appealed to Dewey tended to be pantheistic, closely integrating the divine with the natural universe. His search for an intellectual solution to his puzzles over the nature of the mind, morality, and reality brought him to the third stage of his religious development.

Dewey went to Johns Hopkins University in 1882 to study with philosophy professor George Sylvester Morris (1840–89), whose neo-Hegelian idealism seemed to offer the sort of reconciliation between humanity and God that Dewey sought. In this theistic-idealistic philosophy (not to be confused with Hegel's own metaphysics), God's mind is the ultimate and absolute reality, encompassing everything, including human minds. As functioning parts of God (following that same biological metaphor of the living body and its internally structured organs, tissues, and cells), Morris argued that individuals are always embedded in many larger wholes of varying scope that sustain our growth as Christians. Morris was a universalist, a corporatist, and a perfectionist. All people have an opportunity for salvation; people can become moral through group effort; and each person has a supreme duty to strive for moral perfection.[12] Idealists such as Morris and Dewey frequently and approvingly talked about the "self-realization" of personality—each individual should strive to make real the personal self that he or she ought to become. This kind of idealism still offers a role for God to play, by claiming that God's spirit is becoming realized by each person's progress toward spiritual perfection.

Viewing reality through the metaphor of a living organism guided Dewey as he applied biological concepts to philosophical issues. The evolutionary perspective firmly takes hold on Dewey's thought during the 1880s while he was teaching at the University of Michigan. The Hegelian view of historical evolution emphasizes how the human spirit, manifested in social institutions, is a growing and improving process over time. The Darwinian view of natural evolution reveals how the human brain and its capacities are similarly the product of slow development over time. If religion, too, is an evolving cultural mode of human activity, then religion is really more about humanity's slow spiritual development in this natural world than about a supernatural God's interruptions into the natural world.

From the empirical standpoint of actual human life (and there is no other philosophical standpoint, Dewey regularly proclaimed in his writings, early and late), what does religion actually look like? In Dewey's 1887 *Psychology*, he defines the religious experience:

> Religious experience is the sphere in which this identification of one's self with the completely realized personality, or God, occurs. Religious feeling is, therefore, the completely universal feeling, and with it the progressive development of feeling ends. It brings into our experience the elements which are involved in moral and social feeling, but are not made explicit in them.[13]

The incorporated elements of religious experience, Dewey goes on to elaborate, are the feelings of dependence, peace, and faith. Dewey retained these three factors in his mature naturalistic theory of religious experience (explored later in this essay). The notion of "dependence" became "natural piety"; peace became "harmonization"; and faith became "commitment to ideals." As Dewey gradually lost interest in the actual existence of a divine God, its functions devolved into these three essential factors of human religious experience.

In Dewey's lecture "Hegel's Philosophy of Spirit," he outlines Hegel's theory of the religious spirit.

> [T]he development of religion is that of the religious consciousness, of consciousness which appreciates, at least in the form of feeling, that God is both the subject and object of life; that he is not unknowable nor far-away spirit, but is the spirit of all spirits. In other words, the development of religion is simply the progressive revelation of man to man, the revelation in which man discovers that the ground and aim of his existence is neither in man as a mere individual nor in a world of physical force external to him, but in a living process which unites within its activity him and all other persons, the process of nature itself. The development of religion, in other words, is man finding that the divine

spirit is the source and end of all his activity and that therefore the absolute power of the universe is neither mere blind force nor simply an intelligent person outside of the world, that is, a living spirit who lives in and through the world. (Dewey, "Hegel's Philosophy of Spirit," this volume, ¶153)

Dewey understands Hegel to be claiming that the people *are* the divine revelation and living spirit when they collectively realize and live their common social spirit. By garbing these Hegelian pronouncements in more familiar democratic clothing, Dewey attempted to unify Christianity and democracy.

In this third stage, Dewey decisively favored people's common intelligence: God supplies only moral ideals of conduct, and people have the entire burden of learning how to actually fulfill these ideals in their daily lives. Dewey would no longer permit the universality of Christian ideals to be threatened by denominational strife or God's selective grace. We are all already in God. Jesus retreated in Dewey's religious thought to being only an exemplary teacher of moral ideals. God itself, having no place outside of nature, no salvation work to do, and no judgment to perform, gradually became just a placeholder for our highest moral commitments. God we can do well enough without; what we must pragmatically have to live are shared moral ideals that sustain meaningful lives. Dewey's organic idealism healed the dualisms (saved versus damned, spirit versus nature) of the strict Calvinism of his upbringing and confirmed his preference for universal salvation and his identification of religious faith with moral commitment.

Already persuaded by idealism that traditional empiricism suffers from serious inadequacies, Dewey developed a pragmatic theory of mind and knowledge that emphasized the actively purposive nature of intelligence.[14] Traditional empiricism attempted to account for human knowledge by describing how a lone mind reorganizes incoming information from the senses. In Dewey's new psychology, minds actively pursue information they need to achieve practical goals, and reorganize information for shared use by applying concepts and categories taught by culture. In his *Psychology*, Dewey defines spirit in accord with Coleridge and Hegel: "Spirit is a term used, especially in connection with the higher activities of self, and calls to mind its distinction from matter and mechanical modes of action."[15] Furthermore, following Hegel, a social psychology must replace individualistic psychology. The social institutions of culture, facilitated by language, are responsible for providing life and meaning to our mental functions. Intelligence is essentially social and oriented to group activities.

The implications of a socially pragmatic theory of knowledge for understanding morality are immense and far-reaching. Neither moral ideas nor moral ideals have any significance just because they happen to be in one's mind. Moral ideals cannot be pursued by individuals in isolation and ignorance of one another. Ideals are sustained by institutions that teach them. Therefore, moral self-realization is achievable only where communities of self-realizers are progressing together. Just as Brastow taught that salvation comes through faith, but faith's specific shape must vary widely across peoples due to divergent historical and cultural variations, Dewey saw, again in agreement with Hegel, that ideals are never fixed and permanent but instead evolve within communities.

This theory of progressive self-realization stands opposed to the traditional Puritan doctrine of total depravity, moral helplessness, and divine revelation of commandments. Dewey came to see that although Edwards was right about free will and the locus of moral responsibility, his psychology was quite inadequate for grasping the role of moral ideals in choice. It cannot be a simple matter of choosing obedience or disobedience to some given set of moral rules. Both the traditional Protestant philosophers, such as Edwards, and the liberal Protestant philosophers, such as British neo-idealist T. H. Green, still conceived of moral ideals as supremely aloof and divorced from the average person's faith and intelligence. According to a morality of fixed ideals,

> No moral value attaches to their working-out, or formation. It may belong to the attitude taken towards them, to their choice or

> rejection, but nothing more. But, in our actual experience, no such separation exists between forming and choosing an end of action. Our moral discipline consists even more in the responsibility put upon us to develop ideals, than in choosing between them when made. The making of plans, working them out into their bearings, etc., is at once a test of character and a factor in building it up. But this is an impossibility if the ideal is something given towards which will is to be directed—if it lies outside the normal process of volition. . . . With a fixed ideal, they must lie outside, be mere means, and moral meaning is found simply in the selection of one or other of the ends given ready-made. Deliberation has no intrinsic moral significance.[16]

When Dewey says that deliberation actually does have moral value because it can modify or create ideals, he certainly cannot intend to portray deliberation as somehow suspending volition to survey possible indifferent ideals before selecting one. Deliberation (also called reflection or inquiry) is Dewey's way of understanding how the mind can be volitionally active even while overt action is temporarily halted in doubt about what to do next. Dewey's theory of the process of inquiry in the early 1890s, directly inspired by organic Hegelian idealism, is designed to explain how people are responsible for intelligently selecting ideals to follow in the actual situations we encounter daily.[17] On Dewey's anti-Calvinistic theory, an increase in moral responsibility in a society necessarily requires an *increase* in deliberate freedom exercised by the people.

Having eliminated any need for God's supernatural power, divine authority, moral perfection, or transforming grace, Dewey's organic and pragmatic philosophy was prepared to explain moral responsibility and justify participatory democracy (described in later sections). One problem remained: Was there anything left for God to do? As Dewey proceeded to the fourth stage of his views on religion, the answer seemed to be negative. Indeed, organic pantheism seemed metaphysically excessive, since its unification of God, nature, and humanity remained useful only if God did anything. By the mid-1890s, Dewey had decided that the neo-Hegelian idealism of his earlier years with Morris and the neo-Kantian idealisms such as Green's could not guide anyone toward moral progress because God's moral perfection condemns to complete failure all human efforts. Labeling his philosophy "experimental idealism," Dewey attributed the worth of all intellectual principles and ideals to their practical value for resolving new real-life problems as they arise. Religious ideals of moral conduct must therefore be practical, offering helpful guidance for the growth of moral character.

Dewey's Christian ideals and practical sympathies placed him in close proximity to the social gospel movement, especially concerning its demands for broadening democracy and strengthening social justice. Of course, Dewey had little actual effect on the social gospel movement, since he disagreed with many of its premises. For example, Dewey suggested that inclusive democracy must entirely replace exclusive churches, as churches are only repositories for outdated doctrines.[18] Dewey no longer needed belief in God personally either, and his family had ceased church attendance. No philosophical justification of God seemed possible. Never persuaded that any of the traditional arguments for God's existence had interesting rational force, Dewey did not take such empty intellectual gymnastics seriously. The religious life could not consist of the adoring affirmation of propositions about the divine; something has religious character only to the extent that it motivates and guides a person's general approach to living. As his 1897 lecture "Hegel's Philosophy of Spirit" reveals, Dewey understood and presented Hegel as taking this generally pragmatic approach to religion.

In Dewey's fourth and final stage, one's practical commitment to moral ideals *is* one's religious commitment—God's actual existence is not required. To the objection that many people will commit to moral ideals only if they are sanctioned by a divine authority, Dewey's philosophy responds that accepting ideals on authority is contrary to morality, since such unthinking obedience is the abandonment of moral responsibility. The transition to the fourth and final stage of Dewey's attitude toward religion during the mid-1890s is the complete elimination of God. Only humanity and nature remained. Did this transition mean that Dewey now was a naturalist? Dewey did not embrace materialism when he transitioned from idealism, since late nineteenth-century and early twentieth-century materialism was too crude to adequately deal with the kinds of teleological accounts of consciousness, intelligence, and moral conduct that Dewey's pragmatism required. Nor was Dewey automatically prepared to announce his naturalism, and he did not do so until later on in the first decade of the twentieth century. In 1902 he contributed many entries to a dictionary of philosophy, and defined naturalism in this easily recognizable manner:

> The theory that the whole of the universe or of experience may be accounted for by a method like that of the physical sciences, and with recourse only to the current conceptions of physical and natural science; more specifically, that mental and moral processes may be reduced to the terms and categories of the natural sciences. It is best defined negatively as that which excludes everything distinctly spiritual or transcendental.[19]

Not until 1906 did Dewey explicitly label his philosophy a "naturalism." He took special care to point out how his variety of naturalism forbade science from denigrating or denying our moral capacities and values, just as his naturalism forbade religion from exempting itself from rational criticism.

> For one, I have no interest in the old, old scheme of derogating from the worth of knowledge in order to give an uncontrolled field for some special beliefs to run riot in,—be these beliefs even faith in immortality, in some special sort of a Deity, or in some particular brand of freedom. Any one of our beliefs is subject to criticism, revision and even ultimate elimination through the development of its own implications by intelligently directed action. Because reason is a scheme of working out the meanings of convictions in terms of one another and of the consequences they import in further experience, convictions are the more, not the less, amenable and responsible to the full exercise of reason. Thus we are put on the road to that most desirable thing,—the union of acknowledgment of moral powers and demands with thoroughgoing naturalism.[20]

Dewey's confident application of "naturalism" to his mature philosophy was considerably aided by his favorable reaction to George Santayana's volumes of *The Life of Reason* (1905–6). While Santayana himself was comfortable with the label of "materialism," Dewey immediately grasped how Santayana made ample room for the moral and religious life within a naturalistic framework. In his review of *The Life of Reason*, Dewey stated that "the really vital problem of present philosophy is the union of naturalism and idealism."[21] Dewey's mature naturalism continued to explicitly and firmly distance itself from mechanistic, physicalistic, and reductionistic materialism. By 1910, Dewey no longer had anything positive to say about transcendental idealisms and ceased referring to idealism in general in any positive way. (Dewey's relationship with Hegel's own absolute idealism is quite another matter, as Good's chapter discusses.) Having formulated to his own satisfaction a reunion of the naturalistic worldview with the reality and power of ideals, Dewey avoided Santayana's categorial dichotomy of matter and essence. In his later writings, Dewey instead emphasized the philosophical problem of how naturalism must be reconciled with humanism.[22]

By finding his way toward a humanistic naturalism, Dewey's religious thought attenuated to the moralistic piety of social gospel themes and then openly embraced the secular humanism later elaborated in *A Common Faith* (1934). But Dewey's abiding faith in the human spirit, in the responsible powers of moral intelligence for the social good, was a genuine faith that helped power the progressive movement. By the start of the twentieth century, Dewey joined many religious humanists and religious naturalists in viewing any belief in the existence of a divine power to be incompatible with naturalism and quite irrelevant for a genuinely religious life. Because neither a supernatural authority giving unquestionable commandments nor a spiritual absolute offering inscrutable perfection could guide morality (and they really only obstruct genuine morality), Dewey concluded that liberal Christianity must logically proceed to democracy and atheism. Dewey's atheism was philosophically sophisticated, naturally. Dewey's understanding and sympathy for religious experience, piety, and faith developed in the context of his social psychology and pragmatic theory of knowledge. He recommended natural piety toward the necessary sources and supports of one's life, and he espoused spiritual faith in the possibility of progress toward the highest ideals of moral and political life. When Dewey describes his conception of religious experience, he incorporates both natural piety and religious faith.

We can briefly summarize the continuities between the stages of Dewey's philosophy of spirit and religion, before discussing more details about Dewey's theories of intelligence, morality, and democracy. Dewey's first-stage instinctive trust in democracy and sympathy with universalism developed into his second-stage demand for an integration of our moral and intellectual lives. In the resulting third-stage organic idealism, confidence that all people can morally reason together for social progress provided Dewey with a method for explaining how thoughtful personal freedom and faithful moral responsibility can be socially yoked together for progressive democracy. His fourth-stage humanism concluded that genuinely democratic peoples perform all of the practical functions of God, making all traditional religious doctrine entirely superfluous. Having integrated faith, responsibility, and society, Dewey's mature philosophy offers a unified and coherent theory of religion, morality, and politics. This humanistic naturalism is the culmination of Dewey's search for a philosophy of spirit.

Intelligence, Morality, and Democracy

Rejecting the Cartesian notion of private mental states and isolated rationality, Dewey's evolutionary social psychology instead held that the habits of intelligence are learned by education and modified by further experience in group practices. Three major dimensions of his social psychology, assembled during his years at Michigan and Chicago, shaped his mature philosophy. They are most explicitly developed in *Human Nature and Conduct* (1922) and *Experience and Nature* (1925). First, experience is not subjectively private. Second, people's beliefs and knowledge are not subjective either but instead are functions of purposive behaviors that have socially shared significance for group practices. Third, all knowledge arises from experience, and thought increases the meaningfulness of experience, producing knowledge. Dewey's empiricism held that the techniques of inference that increase meaning (such as logic, mathematics, and scientific methodology) during the process of knowledge production gradually emerge from such experience. Although any learning process is thoroughly dependent on techniques of inference, so dependent that these techniques can in turn appear to be independent of learning, it does not follow that these techniques have always had a separate source or justification apart from experiential learning. Rationalisms and transcendentalisms depend on committing versions of this fallacy. There never was any "pure Reason" divorced from actual lived experience.

For Dewey, both experience and knowledge are thoroughly goal-directed, social in nature, and cultural in significance. Dewey's philosophy could not take either the individual's "subjective" experience or science's "objective" knowledge to be more capable of revealing reality or somehow independent of all-embracing culture. Religion in Dewey's philosophy is similarly treated as an evolving social phenomenon that cannot be evaluated without considering its role in cultural development. The philosophical evaluation of any human practice must be pragmatic.

Dewey's functional psychology implies a pragmatist theory of knowledge. If all beliefs exist to serve the pursuit of practical goals (and not to match some idealized vision of "truth"), then the evaluation of beliefs is judged by finding in experiment how much they contribute to successful behavior. Older theories of knowledge assumed that meaningful mental entities can be easily identified (by the power of reflection?) and compared with the portion of reality to which they refer. Such theories must depict both mind and reality statically, and presume that an isolated internal mental entity has some magical power to perfectly select out the part or aspect of reality that it is trying to represent. However, modern scientific psychology has been dynamic, not static. No scientifically respectable psychology remains to endorse the possibility of the sort of comparison required by a correspondence theory of knowledge. All that remains from medieval and Cartesian rationalism is the correspondence theory of truth, but its remaining defenders happily admit that their theory does nothing to actually assist increasing knowledge. Since pragmatism is primarily a theory of how we increase knowledge, its complaint against truth as correspondence amounts to pointing out its uselessness.

Dewey's *The Quest for Certainty* (1929) explains the regrettable attractions of the notion of certain truth and explains how modern science has replaced it. Pragmatists understand truth in accord with their theory of knowledge. Dewey's pragmatic theory of knowledge is fallibilistic, for it is possible to have knowledge now that later must be modified or replaced by new knowledge. Roughly, knowledge is scientifically justified belief and consists of "warranted assertions." Truth is an irrelevant criterion for knowledge; all knowledge is fallible and revisable. Knowledge is fallible not because some notion of fixed and final truth lingers to condemn current knowledge, but rather because knowledge is empirically warranted and the course of future experience cannot be perfectly predicted. No Gettier-style problems arises for pragmatism because they all require scenarios in which current knowledge is compared unfavorably to some supposed guaranteed truth. Dewey rarely used the term "truth" with approval, and when he did use that term, he was most comfortable labeling as "truths" everything currently known. Dewey's *Logic: The Theory of Inquiry* (1938) most fully develops his theory of scientific method.

Whereas C. S. Peirce's scientific method focused on the natural sciences only, Dewey believed that scientific inquiry's fundamentally creative and experimental method could be applied to all human problems, including moral and political problems. Natural science's conclusions could not erect a new morality, but the scientific method of inquiry itself can be applied to any problematic situation in which current knowledge is unable to resolve doubt about what to do. Of course, our appreciation of our current situation is guided by a vast knowledge base, including principles that emphasize more relevant features of the situation and suggest the best course of action. Inquiry first tries to apply that knowledge base to a problem; failure indicates that further inquiry must experimentally modify the knowledge base. Dewey's *How We Think* (1933) provides his general account of the processes of learning through inquiry. In natural science, this learning eventually implies modifications to theories, whereas in morality or politics this implies modifications to moral or political norms.

Rejecting the Humean instrumentalist model of reasoning, Dewey understands the scientific method as capable of pragmatically evaluating both the means and the ends of actions in light of their further consequences; see his *Theory of Valuation* (1939). Consideration of the means necessary for an end, or of future consequences of achieving that end, is a reevaluation of that end's value and desirability. There is nothing that could be immune from such reasoned consideration, and therefore no end or good can be declared as supreme, final, or all-inclusive. The moral and political life instead requires the constant renegotiation of shifting priorities among innumerable goals, values, and norms.

Dewey regards creative intelligence as necessary for moral responsibility. In his approach to thought and action, the consideration of possible ends and the selection of one to follow are not two separate events (as the outdated dichotomy of reason versus will required) but rather interpenetrating stages in a continual process. In early writings he often claimed that "freedom consists in choosing the moral good." Dewey's mature moral philosophy expands on this notion.

> Reflection presents and weighs alternatives. A thinking being is free in a sense in which no unthinking being could be free, even if fully endowed with "free will." For a reflecting agent can present to himself the consequences of a proposed act; he does not have to wait till the consequences are externally and irretrievably produced to see whether they are desirable or undesirable. If on reflection, the consequences are seen to be adverse, the proposed line of action, if dropped for preference or the bent of disposition, is shifted to some other alternative, which is then weighed. Just in the degree in which one is gifted with the habit of reflection, in

that degree he is capable of acting in the light for a foreseen future instead of being pushed from behind by sheer instinct or habit.[23]

Moral deliberation, like any purposive deliberation, aims at some concrete goal in particular situations. People act for the sake of future outcomes, and explanations of their intentional behavior are incomplete without reference to such possible future events. Since possible future events may not actually occur, this account of deliberation is not a teleological account in the traditional sense, because no future event is postulated as ever causing an earlier event. On Dewey's theory of moral deliberation, intelligence is the range of forethought upon the consequences of various possible ideal commitments. This theory does not violate the Edwardean warning against indifferent or unnatural wills, and it does not transgress modern naturalism's edict against teleological explanations of spooky future causes. For Dewey, moral responsibility is enhanced to the degree that the capacity for intelligent deliberation is enhanced. Such intelligence is exactly the sort of thing that the moral education provided by culture is able to more or less furnish to everyone. This moral education does not, and should not, produce total moral conformity—that is why free communication and intelligent deliberation by citizens in a democracy are still vitally needed to have a peaceful society.

Democracy is Dewey's eventual bearer and genuine meaning of the promise of universalism and self-realization. Dewey's communitarian theory of self-realization (or of the growth of personality, as he usually expressed this concept in later writings) implies that moral responsibility is never truly an exclusively personal achievement (or failure). Moral responsibility, like all cultural capacities, is an acquired function as a person grows into the roles of adult life. This communitarianism explains why Dewey was adamant about his Edwardean point that past external causes for a person's character growth cannot excuse one from personal responsibility. Dewey did not adopt a social psychology and institutional morality essential to a progressive program of social reform only to let personal responsibility evaporate into a maze of mechanistic causes from the past.

In *Human Nature and Conduct* (1922) Dewey clearly explains his view that a person is an agent who acts on the surrounding environment just as much as it acts upon her. With this principle, Dewey can show how moral growth is the growth of a mutual relationship between the self and the social environment. To make space for his alternative approach to moral responsibility, Dewey undertakes refutations of two traditional notions of "social reform" that correspond to the two traditional combatants of libertarianism and determinism.

> There are two schools of social reform. One bases itself upon the notion of a morality which springs from an inner freedom, something mysteriously cooped up within personality. It asserts that the only way to change institutions is for men to purify their own hearts, and that when this has been accomplished, change of institutions will follow of itself. The other school denies the existence of any such inner power, and in so doing conceives that it has denied all moral freedom. It says that men are made what they are by the forces of the environment, that human nature is purely malleable, and that till institutions are changed, nothing can be done. Clearly this leaves the outcome as hopeless as does an appeal to an inner rectitude and benevolence. For it provides no leverage for change of environment. It throws us back upon accident, usually disguised as a necessary law of history or evolution, and trusts to some violent change, symbolized by civil war, to usher in an abrupt millennium. There is an alternative to being penned in between these two theories. We can recognize that all conduct is interaction between elements of human nature and the environment, natural and social. Then we shall see that progress proceeds in two ways, and that freedom is found in that kind of interaction which maintains an environment in which human desire and choice count for something. There are in truth forces in man as well as without him.[24]

Dewey's social progressivism strives to enhance personal responsibility through programs of social intervention (such as education). But by taking either of the two traditional views of responsibility, the idea of "personal responsibility through social intervention" is utterly impossible and contradictory. From the libertarian side, no amount of social intervention could be relevant to the powers of personal choice; whereas from the determinist side, the more that one's society is involved, the less responsibility a person has. Dewey's agent-centered theory of personal responsibility is explicitly designed to be compatible with the social theory that personal responsibility originates and grows only in the supportive context of others in social institutions from the family to the school to the state.

For Dewey, the scientific method applied to society is participatory and deliberative democracy. Like science, which proceeds through distributed intelligence among cooperating inquirers, democracy is the way of life in which mutually respectful citizens intelligently deliberate on their common social problems. *Democracy and Education* (1916) is Dewey's fullest statement of the essential role that scientific, moral, and civic education must play in a democracy. Dewey also sketched a theory of political democracy about the government that would best serve a democratic community. *The Public and Its Problems* (1927) and *Liberalism and Social Action* (1935) develop Dewey's theory of "publics": groups of people with common problems trying to modify social or political norms for remedies. These publics are educated in the skills of cooperative deliberation from schooling and past experience, and compete for attention from elected officials and the whole community with the help of social scientists and other experts. Publics naturally dissolve when their problems are alleviated and people's energies are redirected to other social problems.

Against aristocratic theories of democracy that assign to the government and experts the responsibility for recognizing and solving social problems, Dewey expects greater citizenship skills from the masses so that they can do more than just periodically vote. Of course, if each person on his or her own is expected to help with all of a country's problems, faith in democracy seems hopelessly utopian. However, Dewey explained how ordinary people can devote some measure of time, energy, and intelligence between voting to a few serious problems affecting them, and thus publics can be energized. Prominent examples include unions and civic organizations; national societies such as the American Civil Liberties Union, the National Association for the Advancement of Colored People (Dewey was a cofounder of both), and the National Rifle Association; industry associations; and every sort of lobbying and special interest group imaginable.

If a democracy can promote both the free formation of effective publics and caring responsiveness from the whole body of citizens, then Dewey envisioned progress toward the ideal "Great Community." Democracy is the form of community life and government that peacefully promotes universal moral respect and empowers its citizens, through education, for the civic capacities of moral deliberation. As a regulative ideal, the notion of a Great Community helps expose immorality and injustice, and helps suggest remedies for transforming society.

Dewey, in recognizably Hegelian manner, dissented from traditional liberalism because he argued that people require more than Locke's negative rights and liberties to be full citizens in a unified society. Positive rights to things provided by the state are a necessary balance to negative rights, but in Dewey's view, they are not "positive" enough! The right to fair and safe employment (not just a right to individual property), the right to education in the skills of citizenship (not merely free speech), and the rights to toleration and protection of ethnic heritage (not cultural assimilation and hegemony) are among the additional empowering rights justified in a healthy democracy. Such empowering rights, not reducible to either negative or positive rights, are designed to simultaneously increase the individual's capacities and responsibilities. This increase in genuine freedom (which is far from an increase in mere freedom from restraint or freedom from want) is essential to a democratic society. Echoing and amplifying Hegel's call for the right to recognition and the right to expression of individual personality, Dewey similarly justifies empowering rights by their service in promoting the democratic community.[25] Many of the crucial empowering rights in a modern democracy are also known as civil rights, and Dewey's defense of civil rights during his lifetime rested ultimately on neither human nature nor positive jurisprudence but pragmatic utility for the democratic life.

Dewey's *Ethics* (1908; 2nd ed., 1932), written with James H. Tufts, provides a detailed theory of economic and social justice. Dewey was a democratic socialist because he favored strong democratic intervention in the economic sphere to prevent injustice, but he was never a communist because he rejected its use of violence and he preferred democratically restrained capitalism to autocratically controlled state totalitarianism. Like many liberal progressives, Dewey expected strong unions and other types of effective publics to be able to peacefully negotiate for the things needed for greater social justice. The understanding of democracy as a moral community implies noncoercive deliberation to resolve conflicts. Dewey's view that violence be only a last resort linked him with pacifists such as Jane Addams, who also demanded that governments should engage in international cooperation to actively prevent antagonistic conditions provoking war. Dewey's other major concern was that wars are extremely hazardous to a democracy's civil liberties.

Dewey, like later communitarians (many of whom have also been convinced by Hegel), viewed people as deeply connected to a variety of social groups. Dewey recommended an inclusive cultural pluralism in which people possess group membership while being free to enjoy and adopt other groups' ways. The morality that should be taught in public schools (private schooling encourages antidemocratic tendencies) consists of the civic virtues of respect for the equal dignity of all, cooperative group problem solving, and loyalty to the ideals and aims of democracy.[26] The practical exemplification of these moral ideals in the political sphere constitutes Dewey's understanding of social justice. For Dewey, the personal commitment of each member of a democracy to pursuing these ideals is the proper destiny of the human spirit. From the perspective of politics, a government is just to the extent that the human spirit can achieve its destiny. This is a thoroughly Hegelian stance toward politics. In Dewey's lecture "Hegel's Philosophy of Spirit," we are told that

In the arrangement of classes and the various individuals in the classes, we have the civil order which is conditioned upon justice and its demonstration. Thus there comes into being the State on its external side as government which correlates law as the requirement of the whole with the private interests of the individual. But this government is only the external side of a true organic unity. This constitutes the State where the individual identifies himself with the will manifested in the community in which he lives and thus gets beyond his mere individuality and becomes a member and organ of the whole. The State is then the completed objective spirit, the externalized reason of man; it reconciles the principle of law and liberty, not by bringing some truce or external harmony between them, but by making the law of the whole the prevailing interest and controlling motive of the individual. (Dewey, "Hegel's Philosophy of Spirit," ¶123)

The ethical principle that seems the most firm in Dewey's philosophy, the standard by which he undertakes moral and political criticism, is the demand that all persons must have an equal opportunity to realize their capacities and enjoy life in a manner consistent with the greater social good. However, even this principle remains flexible for Dewey, since the practical meaning of "realizing capacities" will change in the future as the possibilities of human experience expand. Democracy requires a somewhat flexible and experimental attitude toward even our most cherished moral norms and values, because a few may require modification during our lifetimes to permit the alleviation of serious social problems. Even Dewey's own specific formulations of the civic virtues and basic rights are advanced in a tentative manner, and he expected them to be gradually modified in the future.

Piety, Faith, and Atheism

Dewey eloquently expresses his high valuation of religious experience, after it is liberated from supernaturalism, in most of his major works. Unlike fellow pragmatist William James, whose mysticism found divinely inspiring powers present at the fringes of individual consciousness, Dewey required religious and moral experience and belief to have primarily social significance. Therefore, religious experience should consist of one's communion with others in expressions of commitment (through group practices) to social values. In the mid-1890s Dewey argued that a liberal, nonsupernatural Christianity was best for America. This liberal Christianity was still Christianity because the American community still holds Jesus to be an exemplary moral figure of love. For Dewey, the example of mutual love and respect for all people is simultaneously Christian and democratic, and democracy's progress is Christian progress. The preferred alternative to churches and their religions of fixed truth is the "continual revelation" of new truths, arising from the democratic process itself, about how to fulfill the ideal of love.

In *A Common Faith* (1934), Dewey continues to sharply distinguish religions (the churches' doctrines) and the religious (those liberated into pluralistic and progressive democracy), and restates his claim that the democratic experience can also be religious experience. The religious are those who have escaped supernaturalism and sectarian creeds, and can join in the aesthetic appreciation of the pursuit of democracy. In *Art as Experience* (1934) Dewey finds paradigms of aesthetic experience in communal practices devoted to ideals. In *A Common Faith* Dewey again appeals to the coextensive aesthetic/religious experience of pursuing ideals. The democratic commitment to moral respect for all people has the quality of a religious faith, and a democratic culture, like any culture, should possess a religion as a unifying social force diffused throughout all cultural activities. Dewey concluded that the shared aesthetic enjoyment of the democratic community life is collectively of great value, and that this communion can be a kind of highly valuable religious experience.

In *A Common Faith* the notion of natural piety again plays a role. Dewey identified the object of natural piety as the organic unity of human strivings toward ideals with cooperating natural forces. A democracy should likewise encourage this natural piety, and religious devotion is thus properly oriented toward relationships between humans and environment as well as relationships between humans. To the surprise of many, especially Dewey's humanist colleagues, he went farther to controversially offer the label of "God" for the object of religious experience. This came as an especially deep shock to Dewey's allies. Since Dewey proclaimed himself a champion of the scientific and naturalistic outlook, and he had almost nothing positive to say about religion or God between 1892 and the early 1930s, Dewey was known to be a staunch atheist. For example, Dewey was asked in 1933 to sign the Humanist Manifesto. When *A Common Faith* came out a year later in 1934, many humanists felt betrayed.

Critics have pointed out that the name "God" implies at least a unified and purposive agency and perhaps a personality as well, signaling a retreat to older religious notions that Dewey had rejected earlier. Most philosophers and speculative theologians who have pursued Dewey's suggestions toward a naturalistic and humanistic religion remain quite wary of such labels as "God." The task for a Deweyan pragmatism is to explain how the religious devotion to ideals, still useful (and perhaps necessary) in any democracy, can be aroused and maintained without trespassing the boundaries set by naturalism. To comprehend Dewey's pragmatist alternative to a supernatural God, his understanding of the social nature of religion is essential. A pragmatist might, as most did, take the easy option of naturalistic and humanistic atheism. Such pragmatists would simply wait for notions of the divine to become completely absorbed into social ethics and anticipate the coming day when "God-talk" completely fades away. Dewey decided to not be this type of pragmatist. Dewey's mature views on religion are a prominent illustration of the way that he remained indebted to Hegel throughout his long career.

By locating the divine within the human–nature relationship, Dewey's theory of the divine represents a pragmatic development of the Hegelian organic metaphysics that he had sought early in his career. Assisted by his understanding of Hegel, Dewey held during the 1890s that it was Christianity's proper destiny to make its final transformation into liberal democracy. Decades later, in *A Common Faith*, Dewey supplemented this theory by applying the label of God to indicate the holistic way that certain aspects of nature function to support humanity's goals. Dewey approached God in a thoroughly functional and pragmatic way. This approach is evident in his pragmatic tactic of converting nouns into adjectives and then into adverbs. For example, he preferred to talk of "true hypotheses" rather than "the truth," and his greatest preference was to simply speak of "hypotheses that work truly."

This pragmatic appeal to adverbial description works well for Dewey's philosophy of religion. Rather than talking directly about the divine, Dewey described an aspect of nature as being divine, and then preferred to talk about nature behaving divinely. Under what conditions would human beings understand nature as behaving divinely? In 1929, Dewey wrote in *A Quest for Certainty* about how nature is idealizable when it is regarded as a potential aid for realizing human ideals. But idealization must be carefully understood. In all his works, Dewey explicitly refused to endorse any conception of God that makes God responsible for guaranteed ideals and preserved values. In *A Quest for Certainty* Dewey says that a person takes the religious perspective when he or she appreciates how humanity together with its cooperating environment creates a larger whole, having intertwined human and divine characteristics. It only remained for Dewey in *A Common Faith* five years later to use the term "God" to label the direction toward which one's religious attitude is oriented.

To best understand Dewey's long path toward his acceptance of the term "God," we must examine more closely his appreciation for the kind of religious experience that he labeled, probably inspired by Santayana, as "natural piety." By 1934, Dewey stated that God is not just another object inside or outside nature. God *is* nature, when nature is understood as the complex whole of "environment–humanity." On this conception of the divine, the divine would not exist without humanity, and humanity would not exist without the divine. The religious experience is a mature appreciation of this mutual dependency and mutual destiny. Dewey occasionally calls this experience "natural piety" in several of his important writings. In "Religion and Our Schools" (1908) Dewey writes, "It is increased knowledge of nature which has made supra-nature incredible, or at least difficult of belief. We measure the change from the standpoint of the supernatural and we call it irreligious. Possibly if we measured it from the standpoint of the natural piety it is fostering, the sense of the permanent and inevitable implication of nature and man in a common career and destiny, it would appear as the growth of religion."[27]

In *Human Nature and Conduct* (1922) Dewey writes, "The religious experience is a reality in so far as in the midst of effort to foresee and regulate future objects we are sustained and expanded in feebleness and failure by the sense of an enveloping whole. Peace in action not after it is the contribution of the ideal to conduct."[28] Dewey's expression of natural piety appears again in his 1925 *Experience and Nature*. "Fidelity to the nature to which we belong, as parts however weak, demands that we cherish our desires and ideals till we have converted them into intelligence, revised them in terms of the ways and means which nature makes possible. When we have used our thought to its utmost and have thrown into the moving unbalanced balance of things our puny strength, we know that though the universe slay us still we may trust, for our lot is one with whatever is good in existence."[29]

In *The Quest for Certainty* (1929), Dewey says, "Religious faith which attaches itself to the possibilities of nature and associated living would, with its devotion to the ideal, manifest piety toward the actual. . . . Nature may not be worshiped as divine even in the sense of the intellectual love of Spinoza. But nature, including humanity, with all its defects and imperfections, may evoke heartfelt piety as the source of ideals, of possibilities, of aspiration in their behalf, and as the eventual abode of all attained goods and excellencies."[30]

Last, natural piety is prominent in *A Common Faith*, as this selection displays: "Our successes are dependent upon the cooperation of nature. The sense of the dignity of human nature is as religious as is the sense of awe and reverence when it rests upon a sense of human nature as a cooperating part of a larger whole. Natural piety is not of necessity either a fatalistic acquiescence in natural happenings or a romantic idealization of the world. It may rest upon a just sense of nature as the whole of which we are parts, while it also recognizes that we are parts that are marked by intelligence and purpose, having the capacity to strive by their aid to bring conditions into greater consonance with what is humanly desirable. Such piety is an inherent constituent of a just perspective in life."[31]

In these passages Dewey explicitly connects the religious attitude of piety with the religious attitude of faith. By noticing that these two religious attitudes are distinct but also connected, Dewey attempts to distinguish his own position on religion. In the passage just quoted from *A Common Faith*, Dewey says that natural piety is neither a fatalism nor an idealism. Natural piety is directed toward the environing conditions that *partially* control, together *with* human effort, both success and failure. Fatalism, whether arising from theological predestination or materialistic determinism, dismisses human effort as ultimately irrelevant to whatever values may be realized. Idealism similarly has no significant role for human effort, since its romantic orientation toward ideals is admirable yet irrelevant to the guaranteed existence of the ideals. Indeed, from Dewey's perspective, fatalism and idealism are united by their common conviction in the impotence of human effort. Fatalism emphasizes that tragedy cannot be avoided, recommends passive stoicism toward whatever happens in the practical world, and accuses the romantic of false faith in nonexistent ideals. Idealism, in contrast, emphasizes how the human spirit can rise above tragedy, recommends passionate conviction about things outside of the practical world, and accuses the fatalist of ignorance about supernatural values. Ultimately, both fatalism and idealism lead toward moral quietism: a resignation to the seeming fact that no human effort can make a moral difference. Both fatalism and idealism sharply separate faith from human effort: for both, faith should intensify precisely when one's concern with practical affairs must fade.

Dewey's philosophy of religion, opposed to both fatalism and idealism, instead holds that faith in ideals is appropriate only where it energizes one's efforts with practical affairs. Of course our practical efforts will fail more often than not; yet devotion to ideals is religious *because* frequent failure does not extinguish one's devotion. If disappointment with practical efforts instead dominates, natural piety could degenerate into either submissive prostration to the all-powerful or aesthetic absorption with the good, true, and beautiful (or both combined, as in the later writings of Santayana). These degenerate forms of natural piety are not genuinely religious, according to Dewey, no matter how many religions have encouraged them. The only form of natural piety that deserves to be respected as religious is a natural piety toward that sphere of nature–human engagement in which ideals are partially and gradually realizable despite temporary setbacks and ultimate catastrophe.

The frequently heard accusation that Dewey fails to acknowledge the tragic, and hence fails to appreciate religion's power, is made in ignorance of Dewey's sophisticated treatment of religious experience. Dewey is labeled an "optimist" by those fixated by tragedy, as if he felt assured of the eventual victory of human trials, but no such assurance ever appears in his writings. Dewey not only eloquently attests to the tragic, but furthermore, only an approach such as Dewey's is capable of an intelligent appreciation of the full reality of tragedy. Admirers of the tragic who want to go in a quite different direction have only fatalism or idealism to choose from; both paths fail to do justice to genuine religious faith in ideals. In *A Common Faith*, Dewey says,

> Moral faith has been bolstered by all sorts of arguments intended to prove that its object is not ideal and that its claim upon us is not primarily moral or practical, since the ideal in question is already embedded in the existent frame of things. It is argued that the ideal is already the final reality at the heart of things that exist, and that only our senses or the corruption of our natures prevent us from apprehending its prior existential being. Starting, say, from such an idea as that justice is more than a moral ideal because it is embedded in the very make-up of the actually existent world, men have gone on to build up vast intellectual schemes, philosophies, and theologies, to prove that ideals are real not as ideals but as antecedently existing actualities. They have failed to

see that in converting moral realities into matters of intellectual assent they have evinced lack of moral faith.[32]

Traditional religions' demand for their ideals' existence expresses a conviction in the powerlessness of our moral devotion. Instead of energizing moral energy, the demand for faith in guarantees only drains our energy. A few persons, it is true, who believe that they act in accord with the divine way, can feel immense energy for direct action. But since their energy rises in proportion to their conviction in divine victory, they are trapped in a contradiction that can be relieved only by confessing that after all they have been merely an instrument of divine power. The faith of those who instead believe that they might make a real difference themselves is a faith in the worth of ideals regardless of any assurance of success. We are devoted to ideals because of their worth and not because the fulfillment of our ideals is a certainty.

The religious, according to Dewey, do not surrender their ideals and moral convictions in the face of tragedy, and neither do they repose in certainty about guaranteed ideals. The religious do not live in a world where ideals are irrelevant to practical, material conditions. Dewey explained this view to his atheist friend Max Carl Otto in a letter: "I feel the gods are pretty dead, tho I suppose I ought to know that however, to be somewhat more philosophical in the matter, if atheism means simply not being a theist, then of course Im an atheist. But the popular if not the etymological significance of the word is much wider. It has come to signify it seems to me a denial of all ideal values as having the right to control material ones. And in that sense Im not an atheist and dont want to be labelled one."[33]

Although the religious do not believe in any supernatural gods, since they take no comfort in guarantees, the religious are those who are faithful to what is really important: the ideals themselves. As Dewey complained to liberal theologians still seeking a righteous God, either we find God and then commit to whatever he instructs, or we use our prior commitments to ideals to judge which sort of god ought to exist. The first option assumes a sudden ability to forget one's morality and values whenever one thinks that a god approaches (an ability that one should neither want for one's self or one's neighbors). The second option is a frank admission that we are constructing a useless god: if we already have a strong religious commitment to ideals in the first place, adding a god is at minimum superfluous and could potentially lead to the moral quietism of idealism.

> If you appeal to the moral life for your basis and direction, you must be content to derive your conceptions of religion and of God wholly from the implications of the moral life. The question whether there is some physical or metaphysical, some existential, extraneous power working for the realization of moral demands and ideals, is totally irrelevant. To appeal to the supremacy of moral ideals as the ground for the content of religious ideas, including that of God, and then to insist upon a God to give moral ideals external and independent support involves an inherent contradiction.[34]

By this argument, liberal theology must therefore logically proceed to atheism.[35] Of course, Dewey realized that his dilemma for liberal theologians applies to himself. In *A Common Faith* Dewey does not offer a useless god. While Dewey's God neither commands moral rules nor guarantees the preservation of ideals, this God has a pragmatic meaning in the living faith of those who are devoted to ideals in a hazardous universe. Dewey first offers the label of "God" to indicate a set of coordinated ideals to which a person has the highest devotion.

> Suppose for the moment that the word "God" means the ideal ends that at a given time and place one acknowledges as having authority over his volition and emotion, the values to which one is supremely devoted, as far as these ends, through imagination, take on unity. If we make this supposition, the issue will stand out clearly in contrast with the doctrine of religions that "God" designates some kind of Being having prior and therefore non-ideal existence.[36]

Although somewhat different for each person, coordinated ideals are unified for a person in a double sense. These ideals are mutually adjusted to each other, so that the pursuit of one ideal does not demand the violation of another (although adjustment requires that an ideal may never be fulfilled to its fullest extent if considered in abstract and separate from the rest—for example, pure justice won't be possible where love for children is involved). A person's ideals are also unified in the sense that devotion to them brings that person closer to having a unified self.

However intriguing this conception of God may be, Dewey soon revises it.

> But this idea of God, or of the divine, is also connected with all the natural forces and conditions—including man and human association—that promote the growth of the ideal and that further its realization. We are in the presence neither of ideals completely embodied in existence nor yet of ideals that are mere rootless ideals, fantasies, utopias. For there are forces in nature and society that generate and support the ideals. They are further unified by the action that gives them coherence and solidity. It is this active relation between ideal and actual to which I would give the name "God."[37]

Here Dewey depicts a God consisting of the organic whole of human strivings and those portions of nature supporting those strivings. This view of God is neither pantheism nor panentheism, as some Dewey critics and commentators have supposed, since much of the universe will always be coldly indifferent and irrelevant to life. But since part of nature is part of God, Dewey's God is far more than merely one's personal ideals—if God were only that, it would be a personal God indeed! To be religious, persons must experience a relationship with something beyond themselves. Few would dispute this observation. However, Dewey's God exists only because the faithful exist, which obviously contravenes supernaturalism. Yet the God–human relationship was after all designed by Dewey to ensure that God is conceived as living within a social relationship with humanity. In social relationships, people play mutual roles: a person is my friend because I am her friend; that person is my father because I am his son; and so forth.

Dewey's God has objective existence since nature–humanity relations are objectively real and recognizable even by those uninterested in being religious themselves. Dewey's God can be studied and understood, although it will not be the same thing for all people. A close analogy is available in aesthetics: the study of how peoples have used horticulture and terra forming to create elaborate gardens and landscapes in accord with their ideals of beauty. Nature is obviously involved as an active (though unaware) collaborator in such human efforts, and the ideals of gardeners are also available for study (even by those who dislike gardening themselves), since these ideals become evident through appreciation of the work and understanding its purpose. Furthermore, a gardener can enjoy a richly satisfying (while often frustrating!) relationship with nature through gardening, not diminished by the fact that nature's beauty is elicited only through the application of the gardener's own ideals of beauty.

Dewey was well aware that applying "God" to his conception of the object of religious devotion would inevitably arouse controversy. Although Dewey's God has objective existence enough to satisfy the most ardent naturalist, he offered "God" as a name in the most tentative and humble manner:

> I would not insist that the name must be given. There are those who hold that the associations of the term with the supernatural are so numerous and close that any use of the word "God" is sure to give rise to misconception and be taken as a concession to traditional ideas. They may be correct in this view. But the facts to which I have referred are there, and they need to be brought out with all possible clearness and force.[38]

The liberal Dewey was not going to get sidetracked by names for the divine. He sought an idea of God that is at minimum implied by and embedded within all of the world's religions.

> In a distracted age, the need for such an idea is urgent. It can unify interests and energies now dispersed; it can direct action and generate the heat of emotion and the light of intelligence. Whether one gives the name "God" to this union, operative in thought and action, is a matter for individual decision. But the function of

such a working union of the ideal and actual seems to me to be identical with the force that has in fact been attached to the conception of God in all the religions that have a spiritual content; and a clear idea of that function seems to me urgently needed at the present time.[39]

Dewey's resulting conception of God combines essential elements of both pragmatic naturalism and organic idealism. But why use the term "God"? Dewey apparently intended to steal the term away from the supernaturalists and simultaneously tried to distance his religious views from those who want nothing to do with religion. In *A Common Faith*, Dewey explicitly rejects "militant atheism."

> One reason why personally I think it fitting to use the word "God" to denote that uniting of the ideal and actual which has been spoken of, lies in the fact that aggressive atheism seems to me to have something in common with traditional supernaturalism. I do not mean merely that the former is mainly so negative that it fails to give positive direction to thought, though that fact is pertinent. What I have in mind especially is the exclusive preoccupation of both militant atheism and supernaturalism with man in isolation. For in spite of supernaturalism's reference to something beyond nature, it conceives of this earth as the moral centre of the universe and of man as the apex of the whole scheme of things. It regards the drama of sin and redemption enacted within the isolated and lonely soul of man as the one thing of ultimate importance. Apart from man, nature is held either accursed or negligible. Militant atheism is also affected by lack of natural piety. The ties binding man to nature that poets have always celebrated are passed over lightly. The attitude taken is often that of man living in an indifferent and hostile world and issuing blasts of defiance. A religious attitude, however, needs the sense of a connection of man, in the way of both dependence and support, with the enveloping world that the imagination feels is a universe. Use of the words "God" or "divine" to convey the union of actual with ideal may protect man from a sense of isolation and from consequent despair or defiance.[40]

For Dewey to repudiate "militant atheism," when he himself was widely regarded as one of the world's staunchest and most controversial atheists, exposes how his philosophical naturalism is designed to accommodate an earnest and practical humanism. People need ideals to live well, and no naturalism that denies the reality or effectiveness of ideals can be credible in the long run. Nor could Dewey form an alliance with those who prefer the misleading compromise offered by shallow agnosticism.

> "Agnosticism" is a shadow cast by the eclipse of the supernatural. Of course, acknowledgment that we do not know what we do not know is a necessity of all intellectual integrity. But generalized agnosticism is only a halfway elimination of the supernatural. Its meaning departs when the intellectual outlook is directed wholly to the natural world. When it is so directed, there are plenty of particular matters regarding which we must say we do not know; we only inquire and form hypotheses which future inquiry will confirm or reject. But such doubts are an incident of faith in the method of intelligence. They are signs of faith, not of a pale and impotent skepticism. We doubt in order that we may find out, not because some inaccessible supernatural lurks behind whatever we can know. The substantial background of practical faith in ideal ends is positive and outreaching.[41]

According to Dewey, the future of humanism and democracy lies not with agnosticism and skepticism, since these impoverished applications of reason can just as easily erode naturalism and morality as erode religion. The future instead lies with those of faith in the moral capacities of individuals empowered with intelligence.

Dewey's *A Common Faith* argues that intelligent, responsible atheists will still have, and ought to have, religious experiences. Dewey must explain what such religious experiences would consist of, and then he must justify why atheists would want to have such experiences. In response to the first issue, he tells us that religious experiences are intrinsically connected with other essential human activities of value. By defining the religious experience in this way, Dewey points out how the atheist not only can, but inevitably will, have this kind of experience. There is nothing to fear from such religious experiences, because they can be accounted for in a respectably naturalistic manner.

> Separating the matter of religious experience from the question of the existence of God (as for example those as far apart from one another as the Buddhists and the Comtean Positivists have done), I have found—and there are many who will corroborate my experience by their own—that all of the things which traditional religionists prize and which they connect exclusively with their own conception of God can be had equally well in the ordinary course of human experience in our relations to the natural world and to one another as human beings related in the family, friendship, industry, art, science, and citizenship. *Either then the concept of God can be dropped out as far as genuinely religious experience is concerned, or it must be framed wholly in terms of natural and human relationship involved in our straightaway human experience.*[42]

If religious experiences may naturally happen in the course of human social life, even for atheists, what is their function and practical value? Dewey's naturalistic conception of religious experience incorporates both natural piety and religious faith. The "religious attitude" is "a sense of the possibilities of existence and as devotion to the cause of these possibilities,"[43] and while in this attitude, "we are capable of directing our affection and loyalty to the possibilities resident in the actualities discovered. An idealism of action that is devoted to creation of a future, instead of to staking itself upon propositions about the past, is invincible."[44]

Granting that an atheist reasonably undertakes this "idealism of action," why would such effort have a religious dimension? Dewey answers this question by discriminating the essential factors involved in experiencing the intelligent pursuit of ideal ends.

> The actual religious quality in the experience described is the effect produced, the better adjustment in life and its conditions, not the manner and cause of its production. The way in which the experience operated, its function, determines its religious value. If the reorientation actually occurs, it, and the sense of security and stability accompanying it, are forces on their own account. It takes place in different persons in a multitude of ways. It is sometimes brought about by devotion to a cause; sometimes by a passage of poetry that opens a new perspective; sometimes as was the case

with Spinoza—deemed an atheist in his day—through philosophical reflection.[45]

As we have seen, Dewey wanted to label as "God" this process of creating an "active relation between ideal and actual." We must keep firmly in mind Dewey's consistent determination to locate the divine in people's ordinary lives. What precisely is this active religious relation? He expands on his notion of religious experience in this manner:

> The religious is "morality touched by emotion" only when the ends of moral conviction arouse emotions that are not only intense but are actuated and supported by ends so inclusive that they unify the self. The inclusiveness of the end in relation to both self and the "universe" to which an inclusive self is related is indispensable.... Any activity pursued in behalf of an ideal end against obstacles and in spite of threats of personal loss because of conviction of its general and enduring value is religious in quality.[46]

We have asked the crucial question of why Dewey's naturalistic philosophy of spirit would attempt to retain a notion of religious experience and defend its value for atheists. Dewey's answer is that an intelligent and dedicated idealism of action would be attained by people who (1) respect environing conditions on which effective action depends (piety); (2) commit much of their lives to pursuit of chosen ideal ends (faith); and (3) adjust themselves to better harmonize with natural conditions needed to achieve their ends (harmony). If the religious experience is this creative activity of piety-faith-harmony, then Dewey saw no reason why an atheist could deny that such experiences are not only possible but indeed valuable for living a completely secular life-style. Atheists are not radically different from members of religions at the moral level. After all, atheists avidly pursue a wide variety of ideal ends having general scope and enduring value, and they undergo the experience of adjusting their lives to better achieve their ends in the face of potential loss and sacrifice. Furthermore, atheists live in complex societies maintained by devoted political effort.

Dewey found a needed role for religious experience at the political level as well.

Religion, Politics, and the Destiny of Liberalism

Dewey, like many other liberal theologians and philosophers of that time, believed that all religions at their core are moral doctrines and generate moral energy for social reform. As essentially moral in nature, religions instruct the moral expectations of societies, help maintain devotion to moral ideals, and provide an account of humanity's place within creation that justifies those ideals. Pragmatists generally have had little quarrel with these primary tasks of religion, but they have demanded that religions be pragmatically judged by their functioning on these three tasks. Dewey argued that traditional religions can obstruct normal moral development and adult capacity for moral thinking. Traditional religions also sometimes erect unnecessary theological conflicts with scientific knowledge, forgetting their supreme moral responsibilities. Like William James, Dewey sought to describe how religious belief is intrinsically connected with moral conviction. Dewey additionally demanded that religious/moral conviction be continually applied in, and transformed by, the practical arena of civic life.

Turning his attention to his own civilization's problems, Dewey was convinced, with Hegel, that Protestantism's legacy encouraged religious compartmentalization. The strife of denominational pluralism within Protestantism required a partial divorce of civic and religious life. Nineteenth-century liberalism further encouraged this divorce, and twentieth-century liberalism completed it (in, for example, the work of John Rawls and Jürgen Habermas). That sort of liberalism without public religion did not tempt Dewey. To reunite religious and civic life, Dewey argued that Protestant liberalism must be transformed by refocusing on its core moral principles, starting with the Enlightenment commitment to equal liberty and opportunity for all. The moral ideal of universal liberty and opportunity is the foundation for, and justification of, democracy. By demanding that religion in America become compatible with democracy, Dewey was asking only that Christianity return to its true nature. After all, modern Western democracy was no alien import but had developed within a Christian culture.

Dewey's hope for reuniting religious and social consciousness was not based solely on Christianity's potential. When Dewey spoke about the way that a culture's religion can be found in aspects of all cultural activities, he relied on historical accounts of other civilizations and the discoveries of modern cultural anthropologists and sociologists. Based on this large amount of information, modern Western civilization is not normal but is rather an aberration among most other societies, which have had one universal religion. Where Dewey notices other more unified societies, he treats them as the human norm and often adds a tone of admiration. Conversely, when Dewey speaks of his own fragmented culture, he is evidently not proud of its divisiveness over religion. Speaking of his own era in *Individualism Old and New* (1930), Dewey writes,

> The divorce of church and state has been followed by that of religion and society. Wherever religion has not become a merely private indulgence, it has become at best a matter of sects and denominations divided from one another by doctrinal differences, and united internally by tenets that have a merely historical origin, and a purely metaphysical or else ritualistic meaning. There is no such bond of social unity as once united Greeks, Romans, Hebrews, and Catholic medieval Europe. There are those who realize what is portended by the loss of religion as an integrating bond.[47]

But Dewey immediately warns against the seemingly obvious solution of supplying a unifying religion to the people of such a divided society. This method could not be effective because the imposition of any particular religion would seem arbitrary to many, and even if this imposition were done, the bonds of strong social relations cannot be built from mere intellectual assent to doctrinal creeds. The very existence of a particular creed to be adopted is proof of continued disunity. Religious unity is the product of social unity and cannot cause social unity.

> Religion is not so much a root of unity as it is its flower or fruit. The very attempt to secure integration for the individual, and through him for society, by means of a deliberate and conscious cultivation of religion, is itself proof of how far the individual has become lost through detachment from acknowledged social values. It is no wonder that when the appeal does not take the form of dogmatic fundamentalism, it tends to terminate in either some form of esoteric occultism or private estheticism. The sense of wholeness which is urged as the essence of religion can be built up and sustained only through membership in a society which has attained a degree of unity. The attempt to cultivate it first in individuals and then extend it to form an organically unified society is fantasy.[48]

Since religious unity is the manifestation of the degree of social unity, the reunification process has to happen within the field of social interactions themselves, and nowhere else. Of course, no society by definition is completely fragmented. The old social contract notion of atomic self-interested individuals was always a myth. Any society is such because it remains pluralistic while sustaining relationships: its diverse members have overlapping joint interests and cooperative pursuits, as well as inevitable conflicts. A person conversant with the habits of cooperation in his or her society is aware of the factors of social unity. As one grows to adulthood, the norms of social unity are typically internalized and accepted as normal and obligatory. Since normal religious development is continuous with normal social development, people's awareness and acceptance of the more abstract social norms, values, and ideals behind society's habits of cooperation simultaneously show their commitment to a shared religion.

Dewey held a particular view concerning the trajectory and proper destiny of Christian pluralism. After the Protestant Reformation, many European countries accommodating religious pluralism maintained some degree of social unity even while their citizens' loyalties were now divided between church and state. Protestants in England, for example, became more tolerant of Christian diversity so long as loyalty to king and country was assured. America, since early colonial times, has long relied on ideals of toleration, liberty, and equal opportunity to help maintain social unity despite the dispersing energies released by democracy. Dewey concluded that the political religion of America was nothing other than the Christian denominations' common ideals viewed from a political perspective.

To see clearly why Dewey believed that religion and politics can be mutually supporting in a modern liberal society, it is convenient to start with his commitment to education for democracy. Many of Dewey's views about religious experience and education are found in the few articles about religion that he published before 1910, especially his 1903 "Religious Education as Conditioned by Modern Psychology and Pedagogy" and his 1908 "Religion and Our Schools." In the latter article, Dewey argues against including religion as a topic in the curriculum but declares that the schools' proper work is quite religious: "Our schools, in bringing together those of different nationalities, languages, traditions, and creeds, in assimilating them together upon the basis of what is common and public in endeavor and achievement, are performing an infinitely significant religious work. They are promoting the social unity out of which in the end genuine religious unity must grow."[49] In these articles Dewey is looking forward to the reunification of religion in America and views public schools as an essential tool for this work. The primary obstacle is the fragmentation of Protestantism in America, with each church consumed by the notion that God approves of only its particular creeds and ceremonies. The primary condition favorable to religious unity in America is exemplified by the public schools. The public schools help unify all students under some very moral values and political ideals. In Dewey's writings, these moral values and political ideals, such as diversity, toleration, equality, justice, and cooperation, are all justified by the type of pluralistic community that emerged in an immigrant nation such as the United States.

Dewey saw no fundamental conflict between liberal democracy and liberal Christianity. He viewed the growing conflict between conservative Protestantism and liberal democracy as unnecessary and regrettable. Like Hegel, Dewey viewed the Protestant emphasis on the individual's religious liberty and conscience as a highly positive cultural development. Unfortunately, conservative Protestantism overemphasized the individual conscience and the individual's duty to God, placing religious freedom entirely outside the sphere of community conditions and responsibilities. Dewey viewed religious liberty, like all liberties, as organic growths out of successful communities. There are no pre-government or pre-society rights or liberties. Rights and liberties are bestowed by communities in the normal course of social organization. If citizens should have religious freedoms, they must exercise those freedoms in a responsible manner consistent with the community's overall welfare.

In a religiously pluralistic society that has adopted democracy, individuals should have the religious freedom to question and inquire into the community's values and ideals *with the aim* of improving the community's welfare. For Dewey, the improvement of community life is therefore the final pragmatic standard by which values must be compared, reevaluated, and revised when necessary. For too many conservative Protestants, their churches' doctrinal creeds about values supply the final standard. These conservatives believe that the individual's conformity to specific divine decrees about values must always trump the community good, since these decrees sufficiently define what the Good is. Against this view stood Dewey, who was convinced that American democracy works to maintain social unity and promote the social good and simultaneously promotes ethnic and religious pluralism. Dewey concluded that liberal Christianity can still be a positive force for American democracy, so long as we surrender the notion that God is a supernatural king who commands obedience to eternal moral decrees.

What is the democratic alternative to a supernatural God? Following Hegel, Dewey had taken the sociological stance toward religion and concluded that a liberal, nonsupernatural Christianity was best for America. This liberal Christianity was still Christianity because the American community still holds Jesus to be an exemplary moral figure of love. For Dewey, the example of mutual love and respect for all people is simultaneously Christian and democratic. Let us read two quotations from Dewey's 1892 address "Christianity and Democracy." First, he provides his sociological perspective on the genuine nature of religion.

> [E]very religion has its source in the social and intellectual life of a community or race. Every religion is an expression of the social relations of the community; its rites, its cult, are a recognition of the sacred and divine significance of these relationships. The religion is an expression of the mental attitude and habit of a people; it is its reaction, aesthetic and scientific, upon the world in which the people finds itself. Its ideas, its dogmas and mysteries are recognitions, in symbolic form, of the poetic, social and intellectual value of the surroundings.[50]

Second, Dewey announces that beyond proclaiming love, Jesus had no doctrine or creed or church to impose on the world. By offering a universal moral duty of love and nothing more, Jesus did not start a religion, but he did want all of us to become more religious. According to Dewey, we would have to gradually discover how best to love each other over time, in a progressive process of free and intelligent experimentation. "Democracy thus appears as the means by which the revelation of truth is carried on."[51] Therefore, American churches risk betraying democratic Christianity.

> An organization may loudly proclaim its loyalty to Christianity and to Christ; but if, in asserting its loyalty, it assumes a certain guardianship of Christian truth, a certain prerogative in laying down what is this truth, a certain exclusiveness in the administration of religious conduct, if in short the organization attempts to preach a fixity in a moving world and to claim a monopoly in a common world—all this is a sign that the real Christianity is now working outside of and beyond the organization, that the revelation is going on in wider and freer channels.[52]

Although this 1892 address was Dewey's only public exploration of democratic religion until his 1934 book *A Common Faith*, we can see much of the book already contained in Dewey's early philosophy. However, his 1892 address says some very strange things about God. For example, without denying supernaturalism, Dewey demanded that God be "incarnate" in humanity. This demand, expressed here in religious terms, is the naturalistic counterpart to Dewey's philosophical demand, which he understood to be Hegel's demand as well, that any absolute spirit must be actualized in human experience.

As Dewey's political thought crystallized in the 1920s and '30s, he designed his philosophical justification for democracy as both the best type of culture and also as the best form of government. In his justification, there is a crucial role for naturalized social religion—a democratic philosophy of spirit. Dewey embraced liberal democracy's concern for persons, but what should be of primary concern is each person's individual empowerment and capacity for development. He writes: "The democratic faith in human equality is belief that every human being, independent of the quantity or range of his personal endowment, has the right to equal opportunity with every other person for development of whatever gifts he has."[53] For most twentieth-century (and twenty-first-century) liberals, the very notion of a "democratic faith" has paradoxical and confusing implications. Dewey was attempting to confront an emerging liberal conviction, later firmly entrenched during the second half of the twentieth century, that democratic deliberation excludes religious conviction.

Let us look more closely into Dewey's conception, forged during his most neo-Hegelian period, of the crucial role for faith in morality and democracy. Dewey's 1886 *Psychology* expresses his enduring stance that faith is social in origin and significance.

> Both in social and moral relations faith is involved. In moral relations, for example, one says that something must be realized by him which exists not as matter of fact, but as an ideal. The moral ideal is not a mere fact in the world; it is truly an ideal, that which ought to be actual, but is not seen to be so. It is true that morality is not an imagination, it is manifested in living characters in society and the state; but these get all their moral force because they are felt to be expressions of an ideal. This ideal, therefore, not existing as so much fact, must be apprehended by faith. The moral life is one of faith, for it constantly asserts that the final reality for man is that which cannot be made out actually to exist. The religious life only brings this element to conscious recognition.[54]

His 1891 *Outlines of a Critical Theory of Ethics* expands on the social significance of moral faith, and pragmatically directs the whole meaning and value of moral faith toward the welfare of the entire community.

> Moral interest in others must be an interest in their possibilities, rather than in their accomplishments; or, better, in their accomplishments so far as these testify to a fulfilling of function—to a working out of capacity. Sympathy and work for men which do not grow out of faith in them are a perfunctory and unfertile sort of thing. This faith is generally analyzed no further; it is left as faith in one's "calling" or in "humanity." But what is meant is just this: in the performing of such special service as each is capable of, there is to be found not only the satisfaction of self, but also the satisfaction of the entire moral order, the furthering of the community in which one lives. All moral conduct is based upon such a faith; and moral theory must recognize this as the postulate upon which it rests. In calling it a postulate, we do not mean that it is a postulate which our theory makes or must make in order to be a theory; but that, through analysis, theory finds that moral practice makes this postulate, and that with its reality the reality and value of conduct are bound up.[55]

In 1908 Dewey described democracy as fundamentally erected on faith:

> Democracy, the crucial expression of modern life, is not so much an addition to the scientific and industrial tendencies as it is the perception of their social or spiritual meaning. Democracy is an absurdity where faith in the individual as individual is impossible; and this faith is impossible when intelligence is regarded as a cosmic power, not an adjustment and application of individual tendencies.[56]

In 1922 Dewey again connected democracy with faith in the individual.

> It may be that the word democracy has become so intimately associated with a particular political order, that of general suffrage and elective officials, which does not work very satisfactorily, that it is impossible to recover its basic moral and ideal meaning. But

> the meaning remains whatever name is given it. It denotes faith in individuality, in uniquely distinctive qualities in each normal human being; faith in corresponding unique modes of activity that create new ends, with willing acceptance of the modifications of the established order entailed by the release of individualized capacities. Democracy in this sense denotes, one may say, aristocracy carried to its limit. It is a claim that every human being as an individual may be the best for some particular purpose and hence be the most fitted to rule, to lead, in that specific respect.[57]

Dewey believed that democracy's equal concern for the growth of all persons supplies the ultimate moral ground for the superiority of democracy. But he also emphasizes how the capacities of persons and the ways of life people pursue are always evolving (in opposition to conservative theorists who find in some past era the pinnacle of human ability and perfection of life-style). This places great demands on democracy.

> From the ethical point of view, therefore, it is not too much to say that the democratic ideal poses, rather than solves, the great problem: How to harmonize the development of each individual with the maintenance of a social state in which the activities of one will contribute to the good of all the others. It expresses a postulate in the sense of a demand to be realized: That each individual shall have the opportunity for release, expression, fulfillment, of his distinctive capacities, and that the outcome shall further the establishment of a fund of shared values. Like every true ideal, it signifies something to be done rather than something already given, something ready-made. Because it is something to be accomplished by human planning and arrangement, it involves constant meeting and solving of problems—that is to say, the desired harmony never is brought about in a way which meets and forestalls all future developments.[58]

Dewey understood democracy as that form of social and political organization that attempts to fulfill the moral criterion of the genuine community: that all people pursue their personal growth while enjoying the social goods of mutual cooperation that result. Dewey's liberal *and* social democracy bridges the chasm that confronted John Stuart

Mill: How can a desire for the common good be generated from each person's desire for his or her own growth? The bridge is precisely that each person's realization that his or her own good is mostly dependent on the growth of others, and thus it is reasonable to desire the growth of others. In this way, private interests must become public interests. Because democracy should be grounded on the people's reasonable commitment to equal opportunity for all, liberal democracy converges in aims and methods with the moral progress of Christianity.

> [T]he future of religion is connected with the possibility of developing a faith in the possibilities of human experience and human relationships that will create a vital sense of the solidarity of human interests and inspire action to make that sense a reality. If our nominally religious institutions learn how to use their symbols and rites to express and enhance such a faith, they may become useful allies of a conception of life that is in harmony with knowledge and social needs.[59]

In this passage Dewey explicitly provides for the permanent role of progressive churches in a modern liberal democracy. This role has two primary functions: (1) to help maintain commitment to moral equality of all and hence to the faith in human growth that democracy requires, and (2) to serve as a source of social and political criticism when existing social and political conditions obstruct progress toward democracy's ideals. Progressive churches must abjure supernaturalism, because the notion of a divine ruler who mysteriously distinguishes between saved and unsaved practically denies universal moral equality. Progressive churches must instead embrace the only alternative of naturalism in order to be compatible with liberal democracy.

> Lip service—often more than lip service—has been given to the idea of the common brotherhood of all men. But those outside the fold of the church and those who do not rely upon belief in the supernatural have been regarded as only potential brothers, still requiring adoption into the family. I cannot understand how

any realization of the democratic ideal as a vital moral and spiritual ideal in human affairs is possible without surrender of the conception of the basic division to which supernatural Christianity is committed. Whether or no we are, save in some metaphorical sense, all brothers, we are at least all in the same boat traversing the same turbulent ocean. The potential religious significance of this fact is infinite.[60]

Dewey's humanistic naturalism has much in common with John Stuart Mill's search for a religion of humanity. Dewey's concluding sentences of *A Common Faith* echo Mill's call for a religious humanism that is truly centered on the potential for people to take responsibility for, and deserved pride in, the future welfare of all humanity.

The ideal ends to which we attach our faith are not shadowy and wavering. They assume concrete form in our understanding of our relations to one another and the values contained in these relations. We who now live are parts of a humanity that extends into the remote past, a humanity that has interacted with nature. The things in civilization we most prize are not of ourselves. They exist by grace of the doings and sufferings of the continuous human community in which we are a link. Ours is the responsibility of conserving, transmitting, rectifying and expanding the heritage of values we have received that those who come after us may receive it more solid and secure, more widely accessible and more generously shared than we have received it. Here are all the elements for a religious faith that shall not be confined to sect, class, or race. Such a faith has always been implicitly the common faith of mankind. It remains to make it explicit and militant.[61]

By formulating a naturalized religion of democratic faith, Dewey reconciles morality, religion, and politics. Like any compromise, Dewey's religious politics rejects opposed extremes: on the one side, any religion that fanatically elevates the faithful above the rest of humanity and, on the other, any liberalism narrowly focusing on private interests or rights that ignores the rest of humanity. Although deliberately protective of pluralism, Dewey's democracy cannot tolerate any who deny universal moral equality or obstruct the work of advancing human welfare. For theorists seeking a liberal politics so inclusive as to satisfy the religious bigot or the selfish egoist, Dewey's democracy will seem inadequate. However, liberal critics who complain that Dewey's democracy is too narrow are still chasing an impossible liberal dream of a value-free politics; fanaticism cannot be accommodated by any reasonable political theory. Dewey hoped that liberalism could return to its moral foundations, where a genuinely religious faith will always reside.

Conclusion: Dewey's Philosophy of Spirit

Hegel's understanding of "spirit" translates fairly naturally into Dewey's conception of individuality. Dewey's philosophy of spirit is his theory of the social conditions for the growth of individuality. Freedom is the aim and essence of individuality, but not just any sort of freedom is justifiable. Because individuals grow and prosper only in communities, the moral community successfully fosters increasing individuality, and the most moral community is the democratic community. The democratic community, furthermore, is morally justified to all members precisely because their voluntary commitment is primarily to the democratic community's success and not merely to their own private welfare. The democratic community, therefore, is Dewey's answer to Hegel's quest for freedom.

The democratic community's shared commitment to and sacrifice for the ideals of individuality and democracy constitute its religious commitment. The communal experience of faithfully struggling for democracy is a kind of religious experience. In this way, Dewey's understanding of the democratic experience is his answer to Hegel's search for the divine spirit. Dewey's philosophy of religion is not simply atheistic naturalism, although he was a naturalist and an atheist. His broad naturalism makes ample room for the human spirit of individual freedom and moral responsibility. Without this conception of the human spirit, Dewey's social theory of individuality cannot get under way, and his justification for democracy is impossible. In Dewey's thought, his philosophy of spirit is hardly incidental to his overall philosophical project; it is absolutely essential.

REREADING DEWEY'S "PERMANENT HEGELIAN DEPOSIT"
James A. Good

The primary purpose of this chapter is to offer a plausible interpretation of Dewey's 1897 lecture with references to his published writings that provide clues about the permanent Hegelian deposit in his mature philosophy. Before I delve into the lecture, however, I wish to clarify the implicit claim in the title John Shook and I have chosen for this volume, that Dewey has a philosophy of spirit, by discussing Hegel's concepts of "absolute" and "spirit." "Absolute" as a philosophical term is not original with Hegel. From his immediate German predecessors, Hegel inherited the notion of the absolute as a synonym for infinity. Rather than a linear infinity, which raises the logical problem of an infinite regress, Hegel and his German contemporaries understood "absolute" as that which is not dependent on anything external to itself for its existence. Thus when Hegel speaks of "the absolute" in the substantive sense of the term, he means the totality of reality. One might argue that this is not unlike Dewey's use of "nature" in his mature thought.

In *Experience and Nature,* for example, Dewey suggests that nature is logically equivalent to what is actual, but by actual he means whatever occurs in experience. He provides a necessarily incomplete laundry list to illustrate his point. In addition to the physical objects we might normally associate with nature—"stones, plants, animals, diseases, health, temperature, electricity, and so on"—Dewey lists phenomena of social and political life such as "magic, myth, politics, painting, and penitentiaries." Even illusions, Dewey explains, may be illusions, but their occurrence in experience is "a genuine reality." But Dewey's "nature" is also more than the actual because he asserts that even the implicit "potentialities" of the things we encounter in experience are part of nature. Consequently, on Dewey's conception, nature contains "distinct, explicit and evident" objects, but also contains "hidden possibilities . . . novelties [and] obscurities."[1] This bolsters Dewey's earlier claim that nature includes both physical and ideal realities, the latter of which he describes as "esthetic and moral traits."[2] The upshot of Dewey's conception of nature is that it is at once both subjective and objective. Similarly, for Hegel "the absolute" denotes the totality of actuality, but it is also both objective and subjective. Although Hegel, a pre-Darwinian philosopher, left less room for novelty than Dewey, he tried to capture this difficult objective/subjective concept with the term "absolute spirit."

Moreover, like Dewey's "nature," for Hegel, the absolute is a dynamic process rather than a substance. That is to say, the totality of reality, as well as each one of the particulars within it, is known only by its activities, the history of what it has done. Rather than refute the traditional philosophical conception of substance—an uncreated, indestructible, eternal, and unchanging substratum lying behind or beyond the flux of everyday experience—Hegel reconceived reality, the absolute, as process. Similarly, in *Experience and Nature* Dewey asserts, "[W]hen nature is viewed as consisting of events," which he recommends, "rather than substances, it is characterized by histories, that is, by continuity of change proceeding from beginnings to endings."[3]

Hegel also uses "absolute" as a modifier. For example, when Hegel argues that he is completing Kant's project by making idealism absolute, he means that, in order for philosophy to be systematic and thus scientific, it cannot make dogmatic posits. "Dogmatism," Hegel claims, "is nothing else but the opinion that the True consists in a proposition which is a fixed result, or which is immediately known."[4] For Hegel, rational explanation is the very heart of philosophy, and philosophy must not reach beyond itself in order to ground itself; all of its principles must be defended with reasons. Hegel believed Kant had made a dogmatic posit when he invoked a transcendental ego to explain the continuity of human experience and to guarantee certainty within the flux of experience. Another way to state this is that, for Hegel, philosophy cannot appeal to transcendent entities or principles; philosophy's rational explanations of reality must evolve from the subject matter itself, and the philosopher must always resist the temptation to truncate inquiry by positing anything that transcends experience. The moment of "absolute knowing" that Hegel reaches at the end of the *Phenomenology of Spirit* is not complete knowledge of a static being or substratum; it is knowledge that does not seek to go beyond itself in order to ground itself. Upon reaching that moment, one is ready to begin philosophy, which is rational description of reality through the sort of categories Hegel employs in his logic. Rather than a normative logic of reality, Hegel formulated a descriptive logic of experience. Thus when the British neo-Hegelians depict the absolute as a transcendent God or a transcendent realm of logical categories, they make a Kantian move that Hegel explicitly rejected.[5]

In current parlance, Hegel's idealism is absolute because it posits no metaphysical foundation for philosophy.[6] To claim without further explanation that Dewey overcame the absolutism of his idealism is misleading because, to Hegel scholars, it is tantamount to saying Dewey became a foundationalist of some sort. In his 1887 *Psychology*, Dewey spoke of "the perfect personality," which he equated with God, as a way to ground philosophy.[7] In that work, Dewey made the same sort of Kantian move as the British neo-Hegelians. But over the course of the next few years, as he began to criticize the neo-Hegelians, Dewey jettisoned the notion of a transcendent absolute that grounded philosophy precisely because it was a dogmatic posit.[8]

Rather than a move away from Hegel's absolute idealism, this was a move away from neo-Hegelianism and toward Hegel. In fact, Dewey's 1886 "The Psychological Standpoint" rejects foundationalism in a Hegelian move.[9] In that article, Dewey defined the psychological standpoint as the view that "nothing shall be admitted into philosophy which does not show itself in experience, and its nature, that is, its place in experience shall be fixed by an account of the process of knowledge."[10] Hegel makes this point by claiming that "nothing is *known* that is not in *experience*, or, as it is also expressed, that is not *felt to be true*, not given as an *inwardly revealed* eternal verity, as something sacred that is *believed*, or whatever other expressions have been used."[11] Although in "The Psychological Standpoint" Dewey argues that accounting for an object's place in experience is the job of psychology, rather than logic, both Dewey's psychology and Hegel's logic are phenomenological descriptions of experience. In fact, Klaus Hartmann refers to Hegel's logic as a "hermeneutical ontology," an effort to derive the categories according to which we experience the world.[12] This reading is consistent with Hegel's claim that his "objective logic . . . takes the place . . . of formal *metaphysics* which was intended to be the scientific construction of the world in terms of *thoughts* alone."[13] Rather than reject this Hegelian move, Dewey applied it to his own thinking and thus ultimately recognized that it required him to reject dogmatic posits such as "the perfect personality." Moreover, although Dewey ultimately renamed this standpoint "the postulate of immediate empiricism," he never forsook it by positing a metaphysical foundation for philosophy.[14] Thus Dewey's mature philosophy is "absolute" in Hegel's sense of that term. But I need to say more about Hegel's concept of spirit.

At a particular point in history, Hegel argues, the absolute attained self-consciousness or became aware of itself. At that moment of its development, the absolute became spirit. Hegel pinpoints this moment as the point at which man began to write history, which was, in effect, the absolute writing its own autobiography. Spirit gains further self-knowledge and continues its development by reflecting on history because, rather than a substance, spirit is activity. Hegel's "subjective spirit" is the entire range of an individual's psychological life, which manifests in behavioral regularities or habits. "Objective spirit" is a collective term for the totality of the particular beings who have achieved self-consciousness; it is manifested in all of the artifacts, including social and political institutions, mankind has created throughout history. More plainly, for individual humans, objective spirit is the totality of human history. Thus, in Hegel's terms, when Dewey reflects on the psychology of individual humans, in works such as *Human Nature and Conduct,* he articulates a philosophy of subjective spirit; when he reflects on the history of Western civilization, in works such as *Reconstruction in Philosophy* and *The Quest for Certainty,* he develops a philosophy of objective spirit. When Dewey claims that "Philosophy recovers itself when it ceases to be a device for dealing with the problems of philosophers and becomes a method, cultivated by philosophers, for dealing with the problems of men," he is recommending that philosophy focus on the philosophy of spirit in Hegel's sense of the term.[15] Similarly, shortly before Hegel moved to Jena to pursue an academic career, he wrote to his friend Friedrich Schelling (1775–1854): "In my own development which began with the most elementary needs of man, I was necessarily pushed towards science and the ideals of my youth necessarily became a form of reflection, transformed into a system. I ask myself now, while still engaged in this, how to find a way back to the lives of men."[16] Hegel believed philosophy would serve that purpose.

Perhaps most important, both "absolute" and "spirit" reveal Hegel's commitment to holism. Because spirit is activity, rather than some sort of object, and because absolute spirit is infinite, in Hegel's sense of a self-sufficient unity, it does not transcend the particulars of worldly phenomena. Rather, through cognition and practical action, absolute spirit elevates the world to its own level in a continual quest for unity. In cognition, spirit discovers itself in worldly phenomena because a logical structure emerges through the interaction between spirit and world. In this way, logical categories exist within particular things, in a manner similar to Aristotle's conception, but are also bequeathed to particular things by spirit's cognitive activity. Through this activity, combined with practical activity that manually shapes the particular things of the physical world, spirit overcomes its alienation from the world, fashioning a home for itself. Dewey recognized this in a remarkably insightful 1894 letter to his wife Alice: "I can sense that I have always been interpreting the Hegelian dialectic wrong end up—the unity as the reconciliation of opposites, instead of the opposites as the unity in its growth."[17] Rather than absorbing the particulars of everyday experience into a ravenous, all-consuming whole, on this reading, the unity of Hegel's absolute spirit is constantly being sundered and re-created by adversity and diversity (Hegel's "negation"). Hence particular identities are not a mere means to a final state of maturation in which they will be abolished but are the essential engine of its never-ending growth. Thus, in Dewey's many writings on the philosophy of education, in which he characterizes education as perpetual growth, he formulates a philosophy of spirit.[18] Moreover, when Dewey writes that "Progress means increase of present meaning, which involves multiplication of sensed distinctions as well as harmony, unification," he formulates a Hegelian philosophy of spirit in which adversity and diversity drive growth.[19]

My hope is that if readers keep this interpretation of Hegel's "absolute" and "spirit" in mind, our claim that Dewey had a philosophy of spirit, and my examination of Dewey's lecture on Hegel's philosophy of spirit, will make more sense.

Dewey on Hegel's Philosophy of Spirit

Examination of Dewey's lecture "Hegel's Philosophy of Spirit" reveals that the text can be divided into three main sections. The first thirty-four paragraphs focus on Hegel's intellectual development from the time he was born in 1770 until the publication of his first major work, the *Phenomenology of Spirit*, in 1807. In the second section, Dewey discusses the *Phenomenology* for three paragraphs. The third and longest section is a commentary on Hegel's *Philosophy of Mind*, part 3 of the *Encyclopedia*, originally published in 1817.[20] The third section follows the *Philosophy of Mind* so closely that it can be outlined by reference to Hegel's table of contents.

In the biographical section, Dewey draws on three secondary sources, *Georg Wilhelm Friedrich Hegel's Leben* (1844) by Karl Rosenkranz, *Hegel* (1883) by Edward Caird, and an article by Josiah Royce.[21] Dewey's use of Rosenkranz's biography, which has never been translated into English, indicates that he read German rather well.[22] Moreover, because Caird and Royce both relied on Rosenkranz's biography, it is the most significant of the three sources. It is revealing that Dewey did not mention the only other major biography of Hegel that was available in 1897, Rudolf Haym's *Hegel und seine Zeit* (1857). Haym's biography is a key document in the history of Hegel interpretation because it sought to counter Rosenkranz's more positive account and thus contributed to the myth of Hegel as the official philosopher of Prussian conservatism. Because of the politically charged atmosphere in which Hegel scholarship was inaugurated, it is revealing to consider the significance of Dewey's choice of biographical sources.

As one of Hegel's students at the University of Berlin, Rosenkranz is accurately labeled an Old Hegelian. Contrary to popular opinion, not all of the Old Hegelians were right-wing Hegelians. Rosenkranz led the Center Hegelians from his prestigious position at the University of Königsberg, where he held Kant's former chair from 1833 until his death in 1879.[23] Known as liberal reformers, the Center Hegelians were critical of both Prussian conservatism and the revolutionary thought of the Young Hegelians. Rosenkranz was also well known in the United States. An auxiliary member of the St. Louis Philosophical Society, Rosenkranz's writings appeared frequently in the St. Louis Hegelians' *Journal of Speculative Philosophy*.[24] In his biography and other writings, Rosenkranz drew on Hegel's early, unpublished writings, and his short political essays, to depict him as a lifelong advocate of the ideals of the French Revolution, despite its derailment in the Reign of Terror. Like many recent scholars, Rosenkranz argued that Hegel focused primarily on problems raised by the emergence of modern thought and culture. How do we assert and maintain modern individuality and autonomy without surrendering social harmony and cohesion in subsequent terrors? Fundamentally, Hegel was concerned with existential issues raised by the Cartesian dualism on which modern thought was based. Like other thinkers, Hegel believed Cartesian dualism was emblematic of Western man's alienation from nature, society, and even himself.[25] Thus in "Hegel as Publicist," which appeared in the *Journal of Speculative Philosophy* in 1872, Rosenkranz showed that we can better appreciate Hegel's concerns if we supplement study of his major writings with his political tracts, and keep in mind the momentous political events of his lifetime.[26] Although it is difficult to say conclusively from the evidence of the lecture alone, one might speculate that Dewey embraced the moderately left of center reading of Hegel that Rosenkranz defended. Moreover, because recent biographical work on Hegel has vindicated Rosenkranz's depiction of him as a liberal reformer concerned with theoretical issues only to the extent that they illuminate momentous concrete issues, Dewey's depiction of Hegel's intellectual development seems remarkably current.[27]

As a child growing up in Württemberg, Hegel was imbued with a sort of Yankee practicality, Dewey maintains, a disdain for empty ideals that have no concrete effect on the everyday world in which we live. Dewey also compares Hegel to the American Transcendentalists in order to make the point that, in all of his practicality, Hegel had a deep appreciation for the spiritual needs of humanity. Dewey finds three other personality traits noteworthy: Hegel showed an early interest in contradictions, paradoxes, and ironies; he was plodding and meticulous rather than precocious and brilliant in his studies; and he was inherently humble. This humility is manifested by the fact that Hegel was a relatively late bloomer. According to Dewey, Hegel believed that he must disregard his own ideas, remain silent before the subject matter at hand, and allow it to speak for itself.[28] Although this method of study was time-consuming, it was the only way to comprehend things as they really are.

Hegel's method of study is so important to Dewey that it merits careful consideration of Dewey's analysis of its philosophical implications.

> This does not imply a low conception of thought or reflection: it implies rather the highest conception of the value of thought. It implies that thought is so real that it can be found only in the object and not in any subjective opinion. Nor does such a method imply that knowledge is passive,—that the mind is to be merely receptive in knowing; on the contrary, it implies the most acute, the most intense mental energy. It is when mental energy is only partial that we indulge in opinions and arguments. We get part way into a subject and, lacking energy to pursue the quest for the real meaning of the fact, we come to a halt. Then the checked energy relapses into subjective reflection and disputation. The mind has not enough activity to break out of the weary treadmill of its own ideas, to make its way to the fact itself. The highest activity of thought is that which will make itself the pure expression of the facts. (John Dewey, "Hegel's Philosophy of Spirit," ¶4)[29]

According to Dewey, Hegel was not a subjective idealist who reduced material reality to thought; rather, he believed thought is as real as the tangible, material world. Dewey elaborates on this point by explaining that Hegel's "real meaning is that there is no such thing as a faculty of thought separate from things: that thinking is simply the translation of fact into its real meaning; it is subjection of reality subjecting" (¶5).[30] This passage also suggests that Dewey was well aware of Hegel's frequent criticisms of faculty psychology.[31] And Dewey stresses that Hegel rejected the model of the mind as passive spectator and emphasized the importance of "intense mental energy" in the search for knowledge (¶4). The rejection of mind/body dualism, faculty psychology, and the passive spectator theory of knowledge are all prominent features of Dewey's mature thought.

Finally, the passages just cited brings to mind Dewey's frequent criticism of philosophers who stop with analysis of a subject into its constituent parts without seeing how those parts fit into an inclusive organic process. Scholars frequently note that Dewey made this objection in his seminal essay "The Reflex Arc Concept in Psychology"

(1896), which is often hailed as the founding essay of functional psychology. Dewey argues that psychologists err when they view stimulus and response as discrete events rather than as a "sensori-motor coordination," referring to this mistake as "the psychological or historical fallacy."[32] Although the influence of William James's *Principles of Psychology* is clear in that essay, Shook has shown that James was not the primary source for this line of criticism.[33] Dewey's lecture "Hegel's Philosophy of Spirit" indicates that Dewey discerned this mode of criticism in Hegel and that the emergence of Dewey's functional psychology did not require him to reject Hegel.[34] Dewey seems to have believed that Hegel himself perceived and avoided the pitfalls of the psychological fallacy. Whereas Hegel spoke of the limits of the understanding (*Verstand*) and the necessity of seeing the whole through reason (*Vernunft*), in his mature thought Dewey drew on C. S. Peirce's description of the doubt/inquiry process.[35] For both Hegel and Dewey, analysis was a necessary moment of fruitful cognition, but to stop there was to artificially and prematurely truncate the search for knowledge.

After these passages, Dewey briefly discusses Hegel's development at the seminary in Tübingen (1788–1793), where he befriended Schelling and Friedrich Hölderlin (1770–1843), and where his theological studies paled by comparison to the ongoing revolution in France. Dewey devotes more space to Hegel's years as a private tutor in Berne (1793–1796) and Frankfurt (1797–1801), noting that in his early theological writings, Hegel believed the answer to the modern problematic lay in a reconstruction of religion. Dewey correctly points out that Hegel's early theological writings revolved around the issue of church/state relations, which amounted to an examination of the problem of instantiating the ideal (spiritual values and aspirations) in the real (the state).[36] In this part of the text, Dewey describes Hegel's approach to intellectual problems in a way that is rather provocative.

> Hegel was a great actualist. By this I mean that he had the greatest respect, both in his thought and in his practice, for what has actually amounted to something, actually succeeded in getting outward form. It was customary then, as now, to throw contempt

upon the scientific, the artistic, the industrial and social life, as merely worldly in comparison with certain feelings and ideas which are regarded as specifically spiritual. Between the two, the secular, which after all *is* here and now, and the spiritual, which exists only in some far off region and which *ought* to be, Hegel had no difficulty in choosing. Hegel is never more hard in his speech, hard as steel is hard, than when dealing with mere ideals, vain opinions and sentiments which have not succeeded in connecting themselves with this actual world. (¶9)

Dewey's claim that Hegel was a great actualist markedly contrasts with the common characterization of Hegel as the grand metaphysician who reduced the particularities of experience to transient nodes of a dynamic, eternal, and transcendent supreme being. In this passage, Dewey implies that Hegel was essentially a secular philosopher who believed ideas are valuable to the extent that they have effects in the everyday world. Again, this is at odds with the way Hegel is often characterized, not only in textbooks, but also in analyses of Dewey's debt to Hegel. According to Louis Menand, "[T]he attributes of the Absolute that Hegel arrives at working philosophically coincided perfectly ... with the attributes of the God of Christian revelation."[37] This point is telling because Dewey scholars have tried to distinguish his mature thought from his early idealism by claiming that Dewey's rejection of traditional Christianity during the 1880s was part and parcel of his rejection of Hegel. It is implied that Dewey's naturalism, according to which there are no supernatural realities, was incompatible with Hegelian philosophy. This inference would be true, however, only if Dewey embraced the neo-Hegelians' theological/metaphysical reading of Hegel. It is also assumed that Dewey's pragmatic notion that ideas have real effects in the world was at odds with Hegelian philosophy. But Dewey's lecture "Hegel's Philosophy of Spirit" demonstrates that he saw this pragmatic account of ideas in Hegel. As Dewey depicts Hegel here, he was certainly concerned with man's spiritual needs, but he did not see the spiritual as opposed to or distinct from the secular. Spiritual ideals are real only to the extent that they can be fully experienced as real within the secular world.

Dewey's description of Hegel as a great actualist also provides a clue to his reading of the controversial maxim in the preface to the *Philosophy of Right:* "What is rational is actual; and what is actual is rational."[38] Although this assertion has been interpreted as evidence that Hegel supported the conservative status quo in Prussia that existed when that book was published in 1821, the state that Hegel outlines throughout the body of the book is utterly at odds with the reactionary Prussian state.[39] Dewey seems to have understood this claim in a way that is consistent with Hegel's elaboration of it in the introduction to the "Lesser Logic," where he explained that "The actuality of the rational stands opposed by the popular fancy that Ideas and ideals are nothing but chimeras, and philosophy a mere system of such phantasms" and "by the very different fancy that Ideas and ideals are something far too excellent to have actuality, or something too important to procure it for themselves."[40] Hegel's point is that rational ideas actually have effects in the world. At the same time, Hegel was criticizing philosophers' tendency to embrace lofty ideals that have no real import in actual life. Hegel reiterated the point later in the "Lesser Logic": "With such empty and other-world stuff philosophy has nothing to do. What philosophy has to do with is always something concrete and in the highest sense present."[41] The overall thrust of Dewey's lecture suggests that he read Hegel's commitment to the rationality of the actual as a commitment to realism, a commitment to that which actually is, and as a commitment to the practicality of philosophy.[42]

As Dewey continues to discuss Hegel's early theological writings, he maintains that, for Hegel, true religion would unite the self internally and also unite individuals with one another in society—like Hegel's idealized version of Greek society. As Kant and Fichte had seen before him, Hegel saw a role for religion in modern society, but Hegel believed Kant and Fichte both articulated versions of rational religion that would not resonate with modern man.[43] Rather than an abstract religion for philosophers, Hegel envisioned "a natural religion which would unite the reason, avoiding all superstitions, with the positive course of history and the imagination and feelings" (¶13). Dewey writes that Hegel's

> ideal was an organism which would unite in a totality reason and feeling; the world of nature, of the individual and of society. All of Hegel's speculative work grew out of this practical problem, the problem of how a free natural life is possible; how a man can live as a whole, neither surrendering himself to a fixed external authority, nor in his desire to escape this external something, retiring into his own private feelings or into a region of intellectual abstractions. (¶14)[44]

Thirty-seven years later Dewey provided a parallel characterization of religion in *A Common Faith*. The similarity is particularly apparent in the aptly titled chapter, "The Human Abode of the Religious Function," in which he explains that rather than joining a church through intellectual assent to abstract doctrines, a person "was born and reared in a community whose social unity, organization and traditions were symbolized and celebrated in the rites, cults and beliefs of a collective religion."[45] Communal religion cannot be reduced to intellect or feeling, nor can its moral precepts be at odds with everyday practical life. Religion's authority is not external; rather, its authority comes from the heart of the person who has grown and matured within its encompassing social atmosphere. Moreover, when religion is communal, church and state are two sides of our multifaceted social life, rather than opposing institutions. Given their emphasis on communal religion, it comes as no surprise that both Hegel and Dewey were intrigued by the historical development of religion, both within the individual and within society. In the lecture, Dewey discusses Hegel's three stages of religious development, in which the individual progresses from an awareness of his abstract universality, in isolation from nature and from others like himself, to a concrete universality, in which the individual creates a niche for himself within nature and society. In the earliest stage of development church and state may seem opposed, but as we mature we recognize that they are organically related components within the complex fabric of our social life.

Dewey then notes a decisive difference between Hegel and his peers. As Hegel reached the conclusion that the modern problematic required a reconstruction of philosophy, his practicality and his modification of rational religion evince a conception of philosophy different from the conceptions of Immanuel Kant, Fichte, and Schelling. Whereas those philosophers were "more or less professional and academic," building "upon the results and methods of previous philosophic schools," Hegel began by reflecting "upon life itself as he found it in history and upon the main problem of religion, especially as that was related to social development." Dewey does not deny the technicality of Hegel's mature philosophical works, but he maintains that "technical philosophy supplied . . . the . . . outward form of [Hegel's] thinking" rather "than its inner substance and spirit" (¶21). He always focused on the problems of inner and social unity, refusing to reduce the inner life "to an empty spirituality" and refusing to rob the outer life of "deep spiritual meaning" (¶22). Hegel sought to reconcile the immediacy of the Greek polis with the Christian consciousness of sin, the church with the state, and Enlightenment individuality with man's social relations.

To address this problem, Dewey explains, Hegel developed a method that is based on the conviction that thought is not "a subjective faculty" but "the manifestation of the meaning of reality itself." Hegel's emphasis on opposition, contradiction, and negation is essential to this method. Analogous to his three stages of religious development, Hegel's method begins with an "implicit unity," proceeds to an apparent opposition in which "the various elements of the original unity [are] isolated and set over against each other," and ends with "true reconciliation." The first stage can also be viewed as uncritical, dogmatic thought, the second as skepticism, and the third as critical, self-conscious thought in which neither affirmative nor negative are denied but are seen as necessary moments of a developing process. Hegel's method allows for unity in difference, a unified society in which the uniqueness of individuals is not merely tolerated but is essential to society's continual growth, because periods of discord are "element[s] in the process by which the real harmony maintains and extends itself" (¶24).⁴⁶ This point reveals that, for both Hegel and Dewey, rejection of Cartesian mind/body dualism goes far beyond resolving the perplexities of modern epistemology. More than a problem for the formal logician to resolve within the confines of an ivy-laden tower, both philosophers believed Cartesian dualism signified the depth of modern man's alienation from his bodily and emotive self, as well as his world.

Dewey's discussion of Hegel's method is directly relevant to the notion that Dewey had a philosophy of spirit in his own mature thought because of the light it sheds on how he understood Hegel's concept of spirit. According to Dewey, Hegel's absolute is neither a Parmenidean unity nor an aggregate of individuals, because it is an active unity in which the opposition of finite individuals is overcome but at the same time maintained as necessary moments within its ongoing development. Dewey aptly asserts that Hegel achieved this by transforming the dialectical method he inherited from other German idealists with his concept of negation. Dewey explains that "[t]he truth which lay below" Hegel's version of the dialectic "was that all thinking involved, like the process of reality itself, a union of affirmative and negative, or of universal and particular factors" (¶25). Hegel avoids monism, which would undermine the reality of opposing particulars, affirming the reality of particulars by viewing them as the engine of unity: "[I]t is of the very nature of reality . . . to oppose itself and through this opposition to reach its own realized development" (¶27). In fact, for Dewey, Hegel's concept of negation is his greatest insight because it allowed him to account for the unity of reality while moving beyond Schelling's and Fichte's monisms. Schelling reduced reality to "the universal ego itself, the principle of identity in which all opposition of the objective and the subjective was swallowed up," and Fichte reduced it to "the subjective realm of moral action" (¶33).⁴⁷ Hegel "reconciles" Fichte and Schelling "by conceiving of spirit as an active unity in which all absolute oppositions are overcome but in which they are maintained as relative distinctions" (¶35).

Dewey develops this theme as he examines Hegel's relationship to Rousseau, Kant, Fichte, and Schelling. Rousseau's exaltation of the individual, the first moment of a dialectical process, left man isolated and empty. Kant provided the negation by asserting a relationship between the individual and the universal, but he left them in opposition to each other. Fichte's effort to overcome the opposition that Kant bequeathed to philosophy made the moral ideal unattainable because universal spirit could act only to overcome resistance. Spirit emanates the material world in order to have something to overcome, but if it were to overcome the material world, it would destroy itself. Unlike Hegel's system, Dewey maintains, Fichte's is a subjective idealism because it makes the material world mere illusion with "no true objective worth." Schelling tried to correct Fichte by positing "two parallel systems of reality," nature and mind (¶32). The universal ego—the principle of identity—was behind these two systems, but it absorbed all individual identity into an undifferentiated whole, thus denying the reality of the individual. Moreover, for Schelling, knowledge of this original identity came through a mysterious and undefined intellectual intuition.

Dewey's characterization of Fichte also sheds light on why he claimed in the early 1890s that T. H. Green's ethical theory was "falsely named Neo-Hegelian, being in truth Neo-Fichtean." For Dewey, "No thorough-going theory of total depravity ever made righteousness more impossible to the natural man than Green makes it to a human being by the very constitution of his being." Like Fichte, Green had made the moral ideal unattainable. Green did so because he "split the . . . self into two parts," the self that has been realized to date and "the ideal and as yet unrealized self." In so doing, Green committed "the fallacy of hypostatizing into separate entities what in reality are simply two stages of insight." He "stop[ped] with a metaphysical definition, which seems to solve problems in general, but at the expense of the practical problems which alone really demand or admit solution."[48] Dewey's lecture "Hegel's Philosophy of Spirit," in conjunction with Dewey's critique of Green's moral thought, demonstrates that his rejection of neo-Hegelianism during the early 1890s should not be equated with a rejection of Hegel. Moreover, there are other indications that Dewey saw a sharp distinction between Green and Hegel. A year before he gave these lectures, he objected to people who refer to Green as Hegelian: "I never have been able to see any basis for this identification. Hegel protests continuously and consistently against the Kanto-Fichtean ethics, and Green's standpoint is essentially the latter. The logic of the identification of Hegel and Green seems to be: Each is 'unsound' as to the relation of the human and divine self, and, therefore, both teach the same doctrine."[49]

This brings us to the second section of Dewey's lecture, in which he offers a few observations on Hegel's *Phenomenology of Spirit*. According to Dewey, the philosophy of spirit Hegel outlines in the *Phenomenology* successfully rejects Schelling's absorption of nature and mind into an undifferentiated unity that devalues them both, and also rejects metaphysical dualism. Hegel sought a position that was neither monistic nor dualistic by moving beyond the traditional conception of substance; rather than a substratum underlying the diversity of experience, Hegel conceived of substance as an "*activity* to be realized in and through diversity and opposition." Rather than the end of all philosophy, Schelling's unity was the starting point of Hegel's dialectic. In Dewey's words, for Hegel, "The true absolute could be found only when this original identity had differentiated itself and when out of its differences it had reached a unity of life and of activity in which the subject and the object no longer expressed two parallel lines, but were themselves factors contributing to the higher unity of the spirit" (¶33). Rather than substance, Hegel's absolute spirit is subject, and it is engaged in a process of development. The individual things we find in nature are factors within the process, but they are not unreal, as in Fichte's system, because "spirit maintains itself by means of the eternal maintaining of nature in existence" (¶35). Moreover, whereas Schelling's unity is "identity undifferentiated," Hegel's is an identity in difference (¶33).

In all of the technicalities of the *Phenomenology*, Dewey maintains, Hegel did not abandon the problem that initially led him to philosophy. He overcame the Enlightenment's inability to properly account for the relationship of the individual to society. Enlightenment thought so exalted the individual "that law and government were by their nature limitations on freedom and hence, at the most, were to be endured as necessary evils." Yet Hegel maintained modern individuality because his philosophy of spirit gives objective reality "to nature and to the State without thereby making them external burdens upon man's own activity or limits of his freedom." Rather than realities opposed to spirit, nature and state are forms in which spirit realizes itself. In the same way, as an individual develops his own latent spirit, not by vanquishing oppositions as though they are limitations, but by incorporating them into his own activity, he realizes that mastery of "concrete relations of Nature and of the State" allows him to master himself and make himself free. In this way, the individual neither succumbs to external authority, nor does he retreat from the world into his own subjectivity. Through "science, art, religion and state," the individual realizes his unity with absolute spirit without surrendering his individuality and freedom (¶37).

Mind, Morality, and Freedom

Dewey then begins the third section of the lecture, his analysis of Hegel's *Philosophy of Mind*. Following Hegel's organization, Dewey discusses subjective mind, objective mind, and absolute mind, and within each of those major divisions, Dewey closely tracks Hegel's outline.

In his treatment of Hegel's introduction to the *Philosophy of Mind*, Dewey directly addresses Hegel's concept of spirit. Spirit's purpose is self-knowledge, which it gains through the course of human history. In Christianity, men, finite spirits, became aware that their spirits are absolute spirit; in the advances of modern science, spirit has achieved a more complete understanding of itself. When we study the philosophy of spirit, we study "the process by which the spirit works out its true infinity" (¶38).[50] Rather than an independently existing substance "in some external relation to the body," finite spirit "exists in organic unity with it" (¶39); its "faculties" are better understood as "stages in its evolution," or, one might add, functions within the process of its growth (¶40). In the same way, absolute spirit is not separate from the world. As Dewey reads Hegel, absolute spirit is a historical reality; it is the process of humanity evolving in its natural environment. In contrast to the theological reading of the neo-Hegelians, Dewey's is a humanistic/historicist reading of Hegel.

Dewey now begins his analysis of section 1 of the *Philosophy of Mind*, "Mind Subjective." The first topic is anthropology, or the study of "this single developing soul of man" as it interacts with nature (¶54). Like spirit, the soul is not an entity; it is finite spirit before it reaches the level of consciousness. In this part of the lecture, Dewey asserts that Hegel's conception of the soul allows him to sidestep the epistemological conundrum raised by the modern view, Cartesian dualism.

> In strong opposition to this ancient view is the modern one which sets the soul over against nature. It makes a thing out of matter and another thing out of the soul and then asks how it is possible that these two fixed and separate things should have any relation to each other. The question put is, by its very nature, insoluble, and thus we have from the persons who put this problem long dissertations upon the incomprehensibility, upon the mysteriousness of the relations of the soul to matter. The true solution is found when the problem is stated in its true terms. Matter is not one thing and soul another; it is the very nature of matter to come to itself out of its externality, and thus to feel itself, to become internal and ideal. Matter, in other words, is so far from being the fixed, rigid opposition of soul that it must necessarily in its development manifest itself as soul. The soul, in other words, is the truth of matter; it is the real meaning of matter. (¶56)[51]

This passage reveals how Hegel and Dewey sought to reconstruct philosophy. The insolubility of a philosophical conundrum indicates that philosophers have not seen the bigger picture in which supposed opposites are related. Rather than wrestle with such an issue, both philosophers believed that the reconstruction of philosophy required transcending the paradigm in which the old questions were generated.

Dewey digresses a bit from the *Philosophy of Mind* as he addresses an issue that recurs in various forms throughout the lectures, Hegel's theory of causation. This digression is so important that I will digress as well in order to make a crucial point about the Hegelian deposit in Dewey's mature thought.

Dewey seems to draw on Hegel's logical writings when he mentions Hegel's claim that "cause goes into its effect."[52] For Hegel, the understanding sees cause and effect as demonstrably distinct and opposing events, but according to reason "effect contains nothing whatever that cause does not contain . . . [and] cause contains nothing which is not in its effect."[53] At the level of reason, we can see that cause and effect are equally real moments or functions within an organic process.[54] Hegel argues that we perceive a cause only after we see its effect and, we perceive an effect only after we discover its cause: "Both cause and effect are thus one and the same content."[55] This is more than an epistemological issue, however, because a cause is actual *"only in its effect."*[56] Only when a cause produces an effect does it become a cause; thus it is both the cause and the effect of itself. The effect is also a cause, because only when it occurs does the cause become a cause. Hegel's point is that cause and effect are more fruitfully seen as reciprocal moments within an organic process rather than linear relations. For Hegel, this is a more complete picture of causation than one that elevates one element, cause or effect, means or end, as somehow more real than the other. Dewey makes the same point when he discusses the difference between the material world and "the animal organism": "Each member of the animal body is cause and effect of every other: each organ is at once means and ends of every other. All the parts are so penetrated (permeated) by the unity of the whole that nothing which happens in the whole is external or indifferent to it" (¶41). Dewey also explains that even the material world is more fully understood when it is seen as a moment within the organic process of spirit's development.

In the course of his discussion of cause, Dewey makes an argument against materialism much like the one he made in his first published article, "The Metaphysical Assumptions of Materialism," which appeared in the *Journal of Speculative Philosophy* in 1882.[57] Because we know a cause only by its effect, "[t]o say . . . that matter is the cause of soul is to say simply that it is the very nature of matter to become soul, that the soul is the real meaning, the real truth of matter, and this is precisely what is meant by idealism" (¶57). In that article Dewey elaborates on this argument by stating that when materialists claim that matter takes on soul-like functions, they covertly adopt an idealist position that undermines their materialism.

Dewey's attention to Hegel's theory of causation is also apparent when he talks about Hegel's philosophy of history, a subject that Dewey seems to have found especially interesting. Not only does Dewey devote a disproportionate amount of space to Hegel's philosophy of history, he discusses it at several points in the third section of the lecture.[58] In his discussion of the soul, Dewey writes,

> Hegel . . . makes the fullest allowance for the determining influence which the physical surroundings can have upon the human soul. He only differs from Buckle and Draper, who have attempted to trace back all historic events to the influences of this environment in this respect. Buckle and Draper make these surroundings the cause of the conscious states and events. Hegel treats them rather as *factors* in the conscious state. (¶58)

Dewey refers here to Henry Thomas Buckle (1821–1862) and John William Draper (1811–1882). Buckle's most prominent work was his *History of Civilization in England* (1857, 1861), the first two volumes of a planned, but never completed, panoramic history of civilization. It is perhaps significant that a new edition of the book was published in 1897, the same year as the most complete version of Dewey's Hegel lecture. Draper's most important work was *The History of the Intellectual Development of Europe* (1862). Working independently, both men were influenced by the writings of Auguste Comte (1798–1857) to believe that history could become an exact science. Buckle claimed there were laws of history, for example, the law of climate. Similarly, Draper claimed that scientific history should report the ways in which climate, soil, natural resources, and other physical surroundings determine human behavior, as though the causal relationship were strictly unidirectional. Both men believed that physical causes such as climate fully explain the development of nations. Although Buckle's and Draper's books were quite popular during the second half of the nineteenth century, their critics argued that they were generally based on poor research that was selected and distorted to support their preconceived biases about peoples and nations.

By distinguishing Hegel from Buckle and Draper, Dewey makes three important points. First, he asserts that Hegel sees environment as a factor in human history rather than a cause. Environment is merely a factor because, for Hegel, human souls alter their environment, and when they rise to the level of spirit, self-consciousness, they achieve the ability to stake out a place for themselves within their environment by incorporating the materials they find there into their own projects. As Hegel says, each particular human spirit seeks to be "at home with itself."[59] This point is relevant to Dewey's earlier discussion of two "essential characteristics" of spirit: "its freedom and its self-revealing power" (¶46). Spirit's freedom lies in its ability to oppose other things, and even itself, without surrendering its identity. This is spirit's abstract universality, which is equivalent to its abstract, negative freedom. Abstract freedom is also manifested in the will's ability to "identify itself with any particular inclination" (¶103). Abstract freedom is merely arbitrary and subjective. Spirit's self-revealing power lies in its ability to impress "its own identity upon all the material which seems to resist it" (¶46). This is spirit's concrete universality, its positive freedom. Positive freedom is not contrary to negative freedom; it is its fulfillment, because spirit seeks more than the realization of particular inclinations. Spirit seeks "a satisfaction which meets, not one particular desire merely, but all" (¶103). Furthermore, Dewey explains that "Freedom . . . does not remain a mere power of spirit, but the spirit gains freedom as it gains actual power, and it gains this actual power just in the degree in which it transmutes all things into tools of its own action" (¶46).

Second, Dewey notes that Hegel is often accused of "making history purely *a priori*." Many have claimed that Hegel imposed his philosophical and political convictions onto the facts of history rather than letting the facts speak for themselves. Dewey unequivocally declares that this charge "is absurd." Every historical narrative requires unity, a goal toward which it moves, in order to make sense; otherwise, "it would not even be so much as a child's fairy tale, for children require a certain point in their stories" (¶128).[60] Although Hegel's historical narrative is unified, Dewey argues, he does not arbitrarily impose a unity that is external to history.[61] To paraphrase Dewey, in his philosophy of history Hegel remains silent before the subject matter, allowing it to speak for itself. This highlights the difference between Hegel's approach to history, which he also believed should be scientific, from the sort of scientific history found in Buckle and Draper. As Frederick Beiser explains, Hegel "emphasizes that each culture should be understood from within, according to its own ideals and aims."[62] Rather than impose an external scheme of natural laws on history, Hegel's method is to discover historical unity by patiently observing, and then describing, the inner logic of human history.

Finally, Dewey addresses Hegel's theory of causation more specifically. In an apparent allusion to Hegel's notion of the world-historical individual, Dewey averred, "[E]very great historic character is at once made by his times but in turn makes his times" (¶44). Dewey makes this argument for himself in "Time and Individuality" (1940). In that essay, Dewey uses the example of Abraham Lincoln to argue that, although we can speak of the way Lincoln was created by the time in which he lived, this does not logically preclude the notion that he shaped his time. "The conditions did not form [Lincoln] from without as wax is supposed to be shaped by external pressure. There is no such thing as interaction that is merely a one-way movement."

In good Hegelian fashion, Dewey explained that the self is not "something given ready-made . . . in abstraction from time, instead [it is] a power to develop."[63]

These observations highlight a significant portion of the Hegelian deposit in Dewey's mature thought, in which he espouses a Hegelian theory of cause and effect. In *Experience and Nature*, he writes that cause and effect are components of one historical process. Rather than Hegel's term "moments," Dewey asserts that reality is composed of "events." Although we distinguish between earlier and later events, we cannot reasonably assign more value or reality to either: "It is as arbitrary to assign complete reality to atoms at the expense of mind and conscious experience as it is to make a rigid separation between here and there in space. Distinction is genuine and for some purpose necessary. But it is not a distinction of kinds or degrees of reality."[64] In *Art as Experience*, Dewey, like Hegel, espouses an emergent theory of consciousness to explain our ability to think in terms of causal relationships: "Through consciousness, [man] converts the relations of cause and effect that are found in nature into relations of means and consequence. Rather, consciousness itself is the inception of such a transformation."[65] Finally, in *Knowing and the Known*, Dewey's last book, he writes,

> If we watch a hunter with his gun go into a field where he sees a small animal already known to him by name as a rabbit, then, within the framework of half an hour and an acre of land, it is easy—and for immediate purposes satisfactory enough—to report the shooting that follows in an interactional form in which rabbit and hunter and gun enter as separates and come together by way of cause and effect. If, however, we take enough of the earth and enough thousands of years, and watch the identification of rabbit gradually taking place, arising first in the sub-naming processes of gesture, cry, and attentive movement, wherein both rabbit and hunter participate, and continuing on various levels of description and naming, we shall soon see the transactional account as the one that best covers the ground. This will hold not only for the naming of hunter, but also for accounts of his history

> back into the pre-human and for his appliances and techniques. No one would be able successfully to speak of the hunter and the hunted as isolated with respect to hunting. Yet it is just as absurd to set up hunting as an event in isolation from the spatio-temporal connection of all the components.[66]

By this point in his intellectual development, Dewey began to use the term "transaction" for Hegel's dialectical theory of causation. Like Hegel, he maintains that the linear, mechanistic conception of cause and effect is not false. In fact, it is a useful conceptual tool in many situations. It is a mistake, however, to assume that our notion of linear causation is something more than a conceptual tool, or that cause and effect exist as static and discrete realities. When we step back from the immediate situation in which cause and effect were useful, we can see that they are interrelated moments within a larger process of development.

As Dewey considers Hegel's discussion of the feeling soul, he writes that the soul is at one with its feelings. That is to say, Hegel does not discount the value of feelings and the emotional life because, as Dewey maintains, he believed that all conscious life is rooted in feeling. The soul makes no subjective/objective distinction; it is one with nature. "And since the soul is still a unity with nature, it can feel its own qualities only so far as these find bodily expression. Just as a man can make others feel his feelings only as he expresses them by some bodily gesture or outward sign, so a man cannot feel his own feelings except as they come in this round-about way through his body" (¶69).[67] The theme of Hegel's expressivism is intertwined with his actualism throughout the lectures.[68] Just as feelings must find some outward bodily expression, the highest form of which is speech, Dewey writes that we know our thoughts only when we give them objective form in speech or the written word. Thus our thoughts gain "a certain universality of their own" (¶100).

The soul "comes to possess its experiences instead of being absorbed in them" by turning feeling into habit (¶72). Habit liberates the soul from the immediate control feeling has on it in three stages. First, it becomes accustomed or indifferent to certain sensations and "is no longer carried away by every experience." Next, the soul attains the ability to hold satisfaction of its appetites in abeyance. Finally, the soul "comes to possess itself" by developing a habit, that is, a skill. The original unity found in the soul becomes "a *made* unity" in habit. The soul now creates the unity as it gains mastery over the body, which allows it to gain mastery over nature. No longer is the soul inundated by nature in feeling, as habit makes the body "the tool of the soul," particularly in speech, which is "the highest evidence of this fact" (¶73). Habit allows the soul to make the transition to consciousness, and thus Dewey makes the transition to Hegel's discussion of consciousness, phenomenology.

Although consciousness distinguishes subject and object, "the object is always an object of consciousness." Modern philosophy stumbled over the problem of how the world could be independent of consciousness and yet known only if and when it is in relation to consciousness. Dewey writes that Hegel moved beyond this problem by conceiving world and consciousness, subject and object, as distinctions made for specific purposes within "the process of spirit" rather than as metaphysically distinct realities (¶75). Until consciousness fully understands the rationality of the object, it seems external because it is unpredictable and sometimes at odds with spirit's purposes. As spirit comes to understand "the relations which make [the object] what it is," it again becomes one with the object and understands its truth (¶76). As Hegel would say, "The True is the whole."[69] Apprehension of the truth is a matter of understanding the object in all of its relational glory. That is to say, a true statement or idea is one that provides a full account of the object it addresses. To be false is not to fail to provide a carbon copy of the object, but to fall short of a full account.[70] Regularity among the relations is natural law, "a unity which comprehends differences within itself." Notice that, as Dewey reads Hegel, our cognitive apparatus does not impose these regularities on nature, as Kant would have it. "In the consciousness of law, that is, there is the consciousness of a unity which controls both the object and our consciousness of the object" (¶77). The categories according to which we interpret our experience emerge in the process of interaction between thought and object.[71] As consciousness realizes this, it rises to the level of self-consciousness.

Consciousness does not create its objects out of whole cloth, because of "this unity which underlies and controls differences" (¶78). The regularities of nature show us that there is a way the world is, which means that true ideas are ideas that conform to the actual relations in the world. To revisit the distinction between Kant and Hegel, Dewey writes that Hegel's self "is not a formal uniting activity," rather "it is the real unity of the experience itself" (¶81).[72] Yet the unity is not complete until it is actualized in the life of the self. Desire arises because the self has not actualized its unity with the objective world. That actualization requires activity on the part of the self as it learns to make "objects contribute to itself" (¶83). Objects alone, however, can never fully satisfy desire because the self seeks an object that cannot be consumed, a universal like itself. In the *Phenomenology*, this is the point at which Hegel discusses the famous master/slave dialectic; similarly, in the *Philosophy of Mind*, Hegel talks about "the fight of recognition," which is "a life and death struggle."[73] Once confident of our ability to understand the objective world, our inability to actualize our unity with that world leads to self-doubt, which is why we seek recognition from another like ourselves. In this way, Dewey documents Hegel's move beyond epistemology to social psychology.

Dewey discusses the struggle of recognition through which the self realizes the difference between objects and persons and "becomes conscious that he himself is a person" (¶84). The master/slave relationship emerges as one self submits its will to the other in order to preserve its life. The master finds the relationship unsatisfying and counterproductive because he seeks recognition from an equal, not a slave. As the master stagnates, the slave continues to develop, but the complete recognition of "the principle of selfhood" requires a society that moves beyond master/slave relationships to "universal self-consciousness." It is "In this universal self-consciousness [that] the particular self-consciousness learns that it can only be in and through its unity with others" (¶85). At this point, man begins to view himself as part of a larger whole, the community.

Dewey now follows Hegel's transition to psychology, which deals with reason. "This unity of the self and objects, or the discovery that self is the true universal, and that there is no true objectivity excepting in and through unity of particular selves, constitutes reason. Reason, in other words, is a concrete unity of consciousness" (¶85). Once more, reason is a process rather than a mental faculty. The process has two sides, intelligence and will. Intelligence, the idealization of the objective, moves from the object to the subject when the subject comprehends the "rationality of the object," and thus gains knowledge. Will, "the objectifying of reason," moves from the subject to the object (¶86). Dewey's discussion of Hegel's notion of the will shows that he appreciates its subtlety.

> Will realizes the unity in an activity which is neither merely subjective nor merely objective, but in which both the idea and the existing object are included and transformed, thus constituting what we may term either a higher idea or a more adequate form of the object. Will, that is to say, is not merely an act of changing ideas into existences, but is the activity which comprehends within itself as factors both an idea and an object. (¶86)

Dewey places so much emphasis on Hegel's concern about allowing the object to speak for itself that one might ask if he reads Hegel as an empiricist. As Dewey explains, for Hegel, "Sensation is the stuff or material for all knowledge whatever." But Hegel's rejection of mind/body dualism prevents him from being an empiricist in any traditional sort of way. Intelligence does not receive "all its content from without as something foreign to itself" (¶88). Intelligence is always interested and thus attentive to certain elements of its environment; it breaks up the flux of sensation into objects and because it is interested, it brings "a certain unity" to all experience. The actual is rational because at the level of self-consciousness we approach the world as intentional beings. As Dewey explains, "[W]e attend only to that which interests us, and only that interests us which is felt to be bound up within our own being" (¶89). Through attention and interest, sensation becomes perception. Perception "is the state of mind illustrated in the attitude of the poet to some natural object, or of the practical man to some act. The practical man sees into the situation and therefore can tell what should be done" (¶90). When intelligence penetrates into the inner meaning of the object, it makes it its own because intelligence is practical in the sense that it is always engaged in some project.

This brings Dewey back to Hegel's concept of will as he follows the transition in the *Philosophy of Mind* from subjective to objective mind. Although will can identify itself with any particular inclination, in its "struggle for happiness," spirit seeks a satisfaction that will address all of its inclinations (¶103). Christianity addressed this desire by teaching man that the individual is of infinite value, and that he can rise above particular inclinations by recognizing his identity with absolute spirit. Again, absolute spirit is neither a transcendent nor a personal God. "[R]eligion . . . teaches that the divine spirit is actually present in the sphere of the world's existence, that it is the very substance of the State and Family." Absolute spirit is the process of man's development in interaction with nature, and it is known by what it does. The individual must learn to identify with "the absolute will [as] expressed in the world and in social institutions" (¶104). Just as the individual seeks more than the satisfaction of particular inclinations, however, rather than identify with the institutions of a particular community, the individual needs to identify himself with the universal truths of all social institutions. This he does by understanding history, absolute spirit's process of growth or maturation. Rather than acquiesce to the status quo, the individual must work to promote the unfolding of absolute spirit, whose very essence is freedom.

Although man's negative freedom follows from his ability to make free choices, he must realize positive freedom. For Hegel, he can do that only in a society with laws and other institutions that protect his rights. As Dewey explains, "Law and right constitute . . . the objective system of man's freedom" (¶106). Similarly, in the *Philosophy of*

Right, Hegel contends that property gives man "an external *sphere of freedom*" by enabling him to act in certain ways.[74] Moreover, property requires not only that a person take possession of something but also that his or her ownership be recognized. Consequently, abstract property rights are meaningless unless the community recognizes, and thus actualizes, them. With the notion of recognition, Hegel grounds the actualization of rights in the community, without denying that individuals have abstract rights as individuals. Dewey is also interested in Hegel's treatment of contracts, which are perhaps more obviously based on the mutual recognition of two or more parties of one another's rights as stipulated in the contract. As Dewey explains, Hegel did not see conflict as something that can be eliminated from society; contracts both unite and divide individuals because they lead to disputes. People do not enter into contracts because they are "one in their inner being and purpose" but because they have different interests with regard to some external object (¶107). People come together, not in spite of their differences, but because they are different. Rather than an annoyance we must learn to tolerate, diversity is a necessary condition of social progress and unity. In human society then, conflicts are inevitable, and punishment will at times be necessary. Punishment must be more than retribution, however; it must negate the illicit act, and it can only do so by including compensation.

As Dewey and Hegel make the transition to morality, we see that the goal of individual wills is "the realization of the universality of will," or moral unity (¶109). Like Kant, Hegel states that unity is achieved by acting according to a principle that would be accepted by all. Unlike Kant, Hegel argued that this universal moral principle must come from within individuals because every person is a will of infinite value. As Dewey writes, "My every act must . . . be my act, it must proceed from my recognition of what I consider to be good for myself" (¶111). Thus the unity Hegel has in mind is a unity that does not just leave room for individual diversity but that requires it. Moreover, for Hegel, consequences matter because "they re-act upon the original aim, extending it and enlarging it." This point follows from Hegel's dialectical theory of causation in which cause and effect are inextricably intertwined. As we learn of the consequences of various courses of action, we become responsible for considering those consequences as we deliberate about our actions. Similarly, in his 1932 *Ethics,* Dewey wrote that deliberation is "an imaginative rehearsal of various courses of conduct."[75] We formulate a plan of action and then consider the consequences that would follow in order to evaluate the plan. In this lecture, Dewey explains that because "every act . . . reacts upon the interests of the agent," all acts "can be viewed from their relation to the agent's happiness." The agent's happiness is imperative to Hegel, because every individual has the right "to get his own satisfaction and to get it in his own way, not having to take either his ideals or his means from another person" (¶112). This right belongs to every person, and "the happiness of other individuals" is "a social end" for each person (¶113). Individuals have an obligation, however, to "form the best possible judgment of what is right. This control of his judgment by the rationality of the subject matter is what Hegel calls the right of the object" (¶115). Rather than do our duty simply for duty's sake, we must freely choose to do our duty because we fully understand it to be the right thing to do and that it is in our interest to do it. As long as an individual does his duty simply out of conformity to an external authority, including a universal moral principle such as Kant's categorical imperative, he is not at home with himself, and his particular will is not in unity with universal law.[76] As Dewey explains, "Only when the individual will and the universal law are really together does the will find full realization, and the good become an actual fact instead of something which ought to be" (¶116). Once more, for Dewey, the actualization of ideals is the key to Hegel's thought.

The actualization of freedom is possible only in a society whose institutions are rational and in which the individual can feel at home. In such a society, the law is no longer abstract and in opposition to the individual, nor is it merely something "which ought to be." Rather, the individual is able to perform his function in a way that is both fulfilling and liberating. This is Hegel's "ethical world" in which the particular and universal wills are united and in which the individual develops in the family, civil society, and the state (¶117).

Dewey explains that Hegel conceives the family as based on love, which means "each member of the family satisfies himself only so far as he gives satisfaction to the other members of the family" (¶119). The family overemphasizes unity, however; as children mature, they leave the family to assert their own individuality in civil society, which "is the realm of particular self-interest" (¶120). Civil society, "the realm of the system of wants or of industrial society," overemphasizes difference (¶121). But in civil society, the individual can satisfy his particular wants only by providing products or services that satisfy the individual wants of others. Although Hegel speaks of three classes that exist in civil society—substantial (agricultural), reflected (business), and thinking (civil servants)—Dewey acknowledges Hegel's position that in modern society class membership is determined by one's "capacities and inclinations" rather than by birth (¶122).[77]

As Dewey discusses Hegel's philosophy of the state, he rejects the notion that Hegel is an apologist for the conservative Prussian state, but he also voices a criticism:

> This portion of Hegel's philosophy of the state has often been termed simply a philosophical extraction and justification of the then existing Prussian monarchy. While this, perhaps, is saying too much there can be no doubt that Hegel's discussion of the internal organization of the state is the most artificial and the least satisfactory portion of his political philosophy. He makes the ideal State most highly realized in the constitutional monarchy in whose structure simple monarchy, aristocracy and democracy are simply subordinate phases. (¶124)[78]

Dewey does not elaborate on why Hegel's conception of the internal organization of the state is artificial, other than that it concludes with a constitutional monarchy, an unpalatable system of government for a democrat such as Dewey.[79] Perhaps Dewey believed it is artificial because it does not follow that democracy should be a subordinate stage. One could reasonably speculate that Dewey believed democracy should be the conclusion of Hegel's dialectic of the state, but there is not enough evidence from the lecture to say for certain. It is clear, however, that Dewey recognizes the difference in Hegel's philosophy between the government and the state, as well as particular states and the "true organic unity" of all humans (¶123). Rather than a particular government, Hegel's state is the articulated totality of human relations; thus Hegel can consistently claim that it is the *"highest duty"* of the individual to be a member of the state, meaning the human community, and deny that patriotism, "the political disposition," consists in self-sacrifice for one's country.[80]

But world history is the history of individual states, for Hegel, precisely because he rejected the notion that a supernatural force drives history and assumed that all history is human history; that is to say, it is the story of man's self-conscious evolution. As Dewey writes, "[H]istory began only when man came to know himself, when he became a conscious object of interest and of action to himself" (¶131). Individual states have a spirit, in the sense of the spirit of their people, and the world spirit is the spirit of all humanity. Although Dewey speaks in some detail about Hegel's stages of history, in which spirit moves toward the actualization of freedom, that section of the lecture reiterates themes we have already examined. Suffice it to say that, like Dewey's own histories of philosophy, it is a history of man working through dualisms toward a unity of the subjective universal individual and the particularities of his objective social and natural environment. Moreover, it is a history of the unification of what is and the actualization of what ought to be. Such unification and actualization liberate the individual as he continues the struggle to carve out a home for himself within his ever-changing world.

Having addressed subjective and objective mind, Dewey ends the lecture with a brief discussion of absolute spirit, which is realized and manifested in art, religion, and philosophy. In art, the subjective and the objective, ideal and material, are one. And since, as Dewey writes, Hegel conceives absolute spirit as the "completeness of relation in which spirit constitutes both terms," the work of art has "an infinite value." Rather than laboring to communicate ideas in a material foreign to himself, a resistant other, in art man "breath[es] out spiritual life through a medium as plastic and free as [spirit] itself." Although spirit's ideal side can be lost in the state and in history, "In art the spirit exists" rather than "simply striv[ing] to find existence" (¶149). Dewey discusses Hegel's three stages of "the realization of the artistic idea"—symbolic art, classical art, and romantic art—through which man progressively defines his ideas, ultimately recognizing in romantic art that "[t]he material is never able fully to convey the richness of the idea." Hence romantic art works "by suggestion, by delicate hinting, by indicating more than is expressed" (¶152). In this way, romantic art asserts the spiritual above the sensual, which leads to religion. Christianity is the absolute religion because, according to Hegel, its central teaching is that God and man are one, unifying the infinite with the finite, which is "the truth of philosophy itself" (¶154). Rather than elevate man to the level of a transcendent God, in this way Hegel brings God to man on earth by showing him that, taken as a whole, the human race is absolute spirit.

Art, religion, and philosophy have the same content, but philosophy apprehends its content in thought. Philosophy is "that point of view whence we see nature, life and experience as elements in the active process of the self-revelation of spirit to spirit. It is the work of philosophy as such simply to place the dot which ends the sentence, thus for the first time getting the full meaning of that sentence" (¶155). Hence philosophy, as Dewey reads Hegel, is the activity of man coming to know himself through his own historical development. Self-knowledge is not the ultimate purpose of man, however; it is rather a means to the end of man's creating a home for himself by realizing his unity with nature, and the unity of his individual life and experience, within a larger, and perpetually evolving, whole. In this way, Dewey articulates a humanistic/historicist reading of Hegel, in contrast to the theological/metaphysical reading of the British neo-Hegelians.

PART TWO

DEWEY'S 1897 LECTURE ON HEGEL

HEGEL'S PHILOSOPHY OF SPIRIT
1897, University of Chicago

John Dewey

Hegel was a Württemberger, born in Stuttgart in 1770; and if we believe others, the Suabians have certain peculiarities which are not without meaning in relation to Hegel himself. Speaking a somewhat peculiar dialect, they are also marked off as Protestants in Catholic South Germany. They seem to unite a Scotch and Yankee hardheadedness and industry, a devotion to detail, an eye to the main chance in business, a contempt of all idealism that does not succeed, with a certain mysticism of nature. A similar union has been witnessed in our own country in Emerson and others of New England Transcendentalists. Hegel was born of a family of hand craftsmen and minor officials in the Civil Service. His father was in the Fiscal Service and seems to have been more noted for fidelity to his work than for any unusual intellectual ability. Hegel always speaks of his mother with great regard, but she died when he was a youth and not much is known of her.

Nothing striking seems to have marked Hegel's boyhood. He began to keep a diary at about the period when young people usually commence to take an interest in their own affairs. But the three or four years of his record show no trace of sentiment or of introspection, nor yet any important outward act. "Not one thing that could be called an event," says Rosenkranz, his biographer, "appears in his diary." Professor Royce, however, in his recent interesting article in the *Atlantic*, January, 1891, notes two anecdotes which seem of interest as foreshadowing Hegel's later method.[1] They are anecdotes which seem to indicate, even in his boyhood, a certain interest in the contradictions, paradoxes and irony of life. One of them is a record of an occasion when Hegel, as a boy, was eating cherries. A passer-by noted this with some scorn and remarked that young people would not pass a cherry-woman without having their mouths water, but that when one got old one did not care for such things. "From this," says Hegel, "I drew the sad, yet important reflection that when one is young one cannot get all he wants to eat, while when he is old, he does not care about eating that which he can get."[2] The other anecdote is a story told by the rector of the school. It is that he and some other boys were out star-gazing one evening and in wandering about, were overhauled by the police. When explaining their occupation, they were told by the policeman that they should go to bed at night and do their star-gazing in the daytime.

3   Hegel's chief interests seem to have been in his studies. A large part of his diary is taken up with them. Early in his life, too, he began the habit of making analyses of all important writings that interested him. He was apparently industrious and many sided in his studies rather than brilliant. If he had not afterwards gained distinction probably nothing in his youth would seem to mark an unusual genius. As it is, his studies manifest at least one great trait of his philosophical method:—his attempt to get at the natural relations of his subject matter, unperverted by his individual sentiments. Self-effacement Hegel held to be the first law of the intellect. In his discussion of the Pythagoreans, Hegel says that the duty of silence is the essential condition of all culture and learning. We must begin with being able to apprehend the thoughts of others and this implies a disregarding of our own ideas. It is often said that the mind is to be cultivated

from the first by questions, objections, answers, etc. In fact, such a method does not give a real culture, but rather makes it external and superficial. By silence, by keeping ourselves to ourselves, we are not made poorer in spirit, rather by it we gain the capacity of apprehending things as they really are, and the consciousness that subjective opinions and objections are good for nothing, so that at last we cease even to have them. This self-suppression, this silence as to individual reflection, Hegel himself practiced when a boy. This accounts for what seems so strange in one of the world's greatest philosophers, according, at least, to the usual idea of the philosopher; namely, the lack of evidence, that in early years Hegel was a "thinker." This is because from the very first he saw that the suppression of individual thought is the fundamental principle of thinking.

As Hegel grows older, his philosophic method is hardly more than the conscious statement of this early instinct of his. Why is it that individual thought and criticism are to be suppressed? In order that the fact may speak, in order that the fact may be heard out to its last word. Not until the very stones are on the point of crying out will Hegel himself break silence. Not until reality has uttered itself will he speak. This does not imply a low conception of thought or reflection: it implies rather the highest conception of the value of thought. It implies that thought is so real that it can be found only in the object and not in any subjective opinion. Nor does such a method imply that knowledge is passive,—that the mind is to be merely receptive in knowing; on the contrary, it implies the most acute, the most intense mental energy. It is when mental energy is only partial that we indulge in opinions and arguments. We get part way into a subject and, lacking energy to pursue the quest for the real meaning of the fact, we come to a halt. Then the checked energy relapses into subjective reflection and disputation. The mind has not enough activity to break out of the weary treadmill of its own ideas, to make its way to the fact itself. The highest activity of thought is that which will make itself the pure expression of the facts.

I have dwelt on this point at such length because we have in this strain of Hegel's mind a simple and clear illustration of the main point in his philosophic methods:—his insistence that all thought is objective, that relations of thought are forms of the objective world; that the process of thinking is simply following the movement of the subject matter itself. This is often interpreted as exactly the reverse of what Hegel meant. It is often considered to mean that thought as a special faculty of the mind has the power of evolving truth out of itself; that subjective ideas, by some magic, transform themselves into objective facts. But his real meaning is that there is no such thing as a faculty of thought separate from things: that thinking is simply the translation of fact into its real meaning; it is subjection of reality subjecting.

6   From 1788 to 1793 Hegel was at the University of Tübingen in its theological faculty. His life here presents, in the main, only three features of interest to us, first, an inactivity that showed that his theological studies repelled rather than attracted him. The entire instruction was lifeless, rigid and formal; and this apparently both in method and substance. Secondly, he here formed the intimate acquaintance of Schelling, who was to be a great philosopher of Germany; and also that of Hölderlin, a future romantic poet who turned his face towards, and drank his inspiration from, Greek life. The third feature was Hegel's great interest in the French Revolution, then just bursting upon the world. Older heads than those of Hegel and his mates were turned by this outburst for freedom. Klopstock, Schiller and Kant in Germany, like Wordsworth and Coleridge in England, welcomed it as the dawn of a new era. It seemed to be the beginning of a time of freedom, of mutual help and of reason; a time when intellectual formalism, social inequality and political oppression would be swept away. Hegel was a member of a political club and one of the foremost in the defense of the ideas of liberty and democracy.

7   At the University Hegel continued to suppress his thinking. He left the University with a certificate that he was a man of good ability and character, with but little power of speech, fairly well acquainted with philology, but having bestowed no attention whatever on philosophy.[3] This was at the age of twenty-three, an age when Berkeley and Hume had outlined the philosophy of their whole lives.

For six years, that is, from 1793 to 1799, Hegel was a private tutor, first in Berne, Switzerland, and then in Frankfurt. In those six years his philosophic ideas seethed and fermented, and finally precipitated. The first questions which occupied him were concerned with theology; with theology, however, on its historical and social sides. His fundamental problem was the relation of church and state. This question, however, was not to Hegel a problem of external expediency, nor of political machinery; it was the deepest question in life, that of the relation of the spiritual and the worldly sides of man. It was the question of how man's relation to God stands towards his relation to man. The church was the symbol of what binds man and God together; the state, the type of what binds men together.

Hegel dealt with this problem in at least three aspects. First, with his characteristic dislike of the merely vague and sentimental, he contrasted religion with the state, rather to the advantage of the latter.[4] Religion is often interpreted as simply a form of feeling, as a sort of personal experience to be gone through with; and this seemed to Hegel of comparatively little account when compared with the wealth of science, of art, and of social life to be found in the state. Hegel was a great actualist. By this I mean that he had the greatest respect, both in his thought and in his practice, for what has actually amounted to something, actually succeeded in getting outward form. It was customary then, as now, to throw contempt upon the scientific, the artistic, the industrial and social life, as merely worldly in comparison with certain feelings and ideas which are regarded as specifically spiritual. Between the two, the secular, which after all *is* here and now, and the spiritual, which exists only in some far off region and which *ought* to be, Hegel had no difficulty in choosing. Hegel is never more hard in his speech, hard as steel is hard, than when dealing with mere ideals, vain opinions and sentiments which have not succeeded in connecting themselves with this actual world. He thus points out how the religion which consists simply in individual feelings necessarily leads to self-deceit and to a doubling of character. "Its usual form," he says, "is a mode of self-deception in which the person, along with his health and sentiments still retains his usual character. He lodges his usual self along side his spiritual, perhaps dressing him out with flourishes and other tokens of respect. But in conduct and in intercourse, he is the usual self, while on Sundays or among the brethren or before his prayer book, he is quite another man."

10   On the other hand, Hegel points out that the entire means of grace worked by the church, backed by the most full and learned explanations, weigh very little in the scale when the passions, the power of circumstance, education, example and government are thrown into the other scale. The problem, then, which Hegel found on the psychological side was the discovery of that form of religion which would unite in a fertile way the feelings of the individual with the conduct and institutions of every-day life.

11   This union, secondly, Hegel, for a time, thought that he found in Greek life. Judaism was to Hegel a type of religion which divided man from nature and all social relations. It was the religion of an external God and an external law. This externality of law and of God was simply the sign of their separation from all concrete relationships in life. In Christianity, as seen at its best, for example in the life of Jesus, there is a higher principle—that of love. While the Jew would be saved in obedience to an external law, Jesus would be saved by withdrawing all claims to salvation. He claims nothing for himself and thereby frees himself from the realm where law and punishment have meaning. There is no law to regulate and restrain personal desires, because there are no merely personal desires. There is no punishment, not because the external result of evil is done away with, for that must follow action, but because that person accepts with love that very punishment. Being reconciled to punishment, it ceases to be punishment. Forgiveness of sins is fate reconciled to love, Hegel says. But this freedom from law and guilt has been at the expense of all the positive interests of life. The very attempt to escape from the fate of all finite things brings the entire fate of the finite upon Jesus. He has the guilt of innocence. Hegel means by this that the principle of love is indeed a principle of unity, but a unity made by keeping out of, by denying all the specific relations of the world, and thus the world is set against it. The principle of the church thus becomes that

of a society of men who, remote from the world, are engaged in the service of God. "Between the extremes of friendship, hate or indifference toward the world, between these extremes which are the necessary results of the opposition of God and the world, the Christian has had its circle, now forwards, now backwards; but it is its fate that church and state, service of God and love, piety and virtue, spiritual and secular action, can never unite into one."

The Greek conception of the relation of church and state was then more satisfactory to Hegel than either the Jewish or the Christian. "To the Greek, the idea of the fatherland, the State,[5] was the invisible, the higher reality, for which he laboured, and his constant motive."[6] (Caird) Religion centered in and about the state. It was only the idealization of the interests which made up the actual social and political life of the Greek. In Greece there was no division, no divorce of the worldly and the spiritual, of piety and virtue. Man lived a single, concrete life in which science, art, religion and politics were as one.

The other phase of Hegel's interest in church and state had a more directly philosophical origin. Kant and, following him, Fichte, had endeavored to establish the conception of a purely rational religion, a religion which was the outgrowth of rational ethics. They thought that within the ethical ideas themselves there could be found a basis for the conception of God and immortality. The religion of History and of positive worship meant little or nothing to them. Indeed, this was the period of the Enlightenment, of the Aufklärung that is, of extreme rationalism. The conception of miracle and of external revelation had no hold upon the educated classes. Kant accepted the intellectual results of the Enlightenment so far as they were negative to the supernatural religion, but endeavored on its ruin to establish a rational religion. Hegel both agreed with and differed from this prevalent rationalism. In agreement with it he distinguished between a fetish and a rational faith. And yet the formulae of rationalism Hegel found to be mere babbling, and the peddling of stale panaceas. The current rationalism, even that of Kant, was abstract; it took no account of historical development. It made of no value the feelings, the desires, or the sensuous side of man. It was a religion only for philosophers, and for them only in the region of intellectual abstractions. As against this abstract religion, Hegel conceived a natural religion which would unite the reason, avoiding all superstitions, with the positive course of history and the imagination and feelings.

14   We thus have before us the stage of Hegel's reflection. His ideal was an organism which would unite in a totality reason and feeling; the world of nature, of the individual and of society. All of Hegel's speculative work grew out of this practical problem, the problem of how a free natural life is possible; how a man can live as a whole, neither surrendering himself to a fixed external authority, nor in his desire to escape this external something, retiring into his own private feelings or into a region of intellectual abstractions. Upon the whole, Hegel is as yet more conscious of the problem than of its solution. He is more aware of the oppositions which must needs be reconciled than of the unity which says the solvent word.[7]

15   Two thoughts commend themselves most favorably to him. One speculative, the idea of love as the unity which reconciles all differences, a unity which must go forth of itself, and yet which in its outgoing only manifests and confirms itself. The other thought was historical, the idea of the Greek life as the true life, the life which made[8] no breach between God and nature, nature and man.

16   In the last two years of this period, we find Hegel advancing to a more positive solution and by 1800 he had worked out in outline the whole of his future system. The keynote to his thought we find in a comment which he makes upon Kant's "Theory of the Law."[9] He summed up Kant's position as follows: The Church and the State must leave each other in peace, they must have nothing to do with each other. Hegel goes on to ask how far this division is possible. If the State is simply a secular organization, based upon natural wants, and limited to securing and protecting property, then it stands below and opposite the Church; for the Church deals with man, not simply as a property owner, but in his whole being. The object of the Church is to give man, and to maintain in him, the sense of his completeness. A man acting according to the spirit of the Church must therefore act against the very nature of the State. "In truth," says Hegel, "no

one except the Jesuits and the Quakers really act upon this conception of the division of the Church and the State. If the principle of the State is itself complete and whole, it is impossible that Church and State should be divided. The totality which belongs to the Church is only a fragment when man is split up into a secular and spiritual being." Hegel adds, "The very same totality that belongs to the State in thought and as a controlling law also belongs to the Church in imagination and life." Hegel, in other words, is now convinced that Church and State, as man's social relationships, and his connection with the absolute unity of life, are only two sides of the same fact. On one side we have the truth in the form of imagination, feeling, art; on the other, in the form of understanding and philosophy. Hegel at this period placed religion higher than philosophy on the ground that thought can never get beyond a certain abstraction, and that therefore its result was to set the finite over against the infinite, even when pointing out the necessity of their union. The unity which to thought was only an ideal to be reached, in the actual life of religion and art, was realized.

Hegel's thought during his two years of residence at Frankfurt is simply a working out of the opposition and yet necessary relation between the finite and the infinite. We may trace this development in the sketch of his philosophy written in 1799 or 1800, especially in that part of it which deals with the development of the religious idea. Hegel now conceives of three periods in the working of man's religious consciousness. First, the period of the unconscious union of the infinite and the finite. The object of all religion is to reconcile the Divine and the human. In the first period, the reconciliation is direct and natural. There is unity, because as yet no separation has been conceived of; nature is itself divine. No element of the world or of man has parted from God. The daily affairs of life are a conversation with God, a mutual giving and taking, and every daily event is a pregnant word of divine faith. But this direct unity must pass away. It exists only because man is not yet conscious of himself. It is a union of art, of the imagination and the feelings, rather than of developed thought. When man's spirit comes to the consciousness of its own universal character, it must necessarily abandon its dwelling place in nature and elevate itself above nature. It conceives of itself as universal, in comparison with which everything in nature is only particular. This break in man's life has two sides:—on one side, it is the consciousness of personality that I am I, as against the world and every other individual. This is the universal side, but it is purely empty; it has lost all definite relation to nature and to other men. It is a bare, empty self-assertion. In this universal self, which has no special content, lie the contradictions of man's life. It is a time of the consciousness of sin and of the weight of law. It is a time of infinite pain. A consciousness of the universal which should be everything and yet is nothing is man's consciousness of his isolation and of his guilt. Without this consciousness of his own universal nature, man would not be aware of the divine spirit present within him and thus could have no consciousness of law or of sin.

18   But in the very depth of this consciousness of sin there is involved a higher principle of unity than was to be found in Greek life. In his practical consciousness of himself as distinct from and set over against Nature and the State, man is conscious of his unity with God. This truth is expressed in Christ. In taking upon himself the pain of the separation of all concrete relationships, Jesus realized his unity with God and thus infinite pain was transformed into infinite joy. The suffering of the isolation and of the joy of complete union were but the negative and the positive sides of the same thing. Man's very consciousness of his isolation, the negative side, was in reality but the dawning consciousness of a higher union than before known. These two sides of man's life, his consciousness of sin on one side, that is, his consciousness of separation from all definite relations, and his consciousness of redemption on the other, Hegel found symbolized in the crucifixion and resurrection.

19   This consciousness of separation from nature and of the possibility of a higher unity, that is, that afforded by nature, is the second period of religious development. The third period comes when the spirit, now conscious of its universal and divine nature, works upon the external world and elevates it to its own level. We thus have again, as

in the first period, a union of nature and spirit; not, however, an immediate union, but one which has been worked out, which has been made by the spirit itself. It is realized that the breach is not really between Nature and the Spirit, but is rather within the Spirit itself, between its consciousness of its own universal character and the actual lack of such universality on its objective side. This breach is overcome just so far as man's spirit, by science, by art and by invention, makes nature the expression of his own purposes and ideals.

By man again consecrated, all nature is also made holy, a temple of renewed life. To everything is given a new consecration; to every act and to everything from the highest to the lowest that divinity which has been lost is given back. The old curse laid upon everything is dissolved. All nature becomes gracious again and in its pain is reconciled. Man, who has been cut off from Nature, becomes the point of union between Nature and God. The spirit now has a true universality, a universality which maintains itself in the whole process of life.

At this point we may sum up Hegel's thought as it now stands. First, as to the main course of his philosophic interest. His chief interest was practical rather than merely theoretical. His philosophic problem and speculations had not grown up through a study of the previous philosophers. Kant's philosophic interest was from the first somewhat technical in character. It was more or less professional and academic. He built upon the results and methods of previous philosophic schools. The same may be said in general of Fichte and of Schelling. Hegel had first reflected upon life itself as he found it in history and upon the main problem of religion, especially as that was related to social development. His interest in philosophic work went, indeed, hand in hand with his more general studies; but technical philosophy supplied rather the mould and outward form of his thinking than its inner substance and spirit. It gave him his terminology and the formal side of his method and of his mode of statement. But after all, Hegel was mainly concerned with the problem of the unity of life. The questions of the unity of thought and of the unity of

Nature were of interest to him on account of their connection with this practical question. Of course, the special ways in which Hegel looked at this problem of the unity of life was fixed for him by certain more or less definite historic and philosophic problems. There was, for example, the question of how the principles of the Greek and Christian theories of life could be reconciled; how the idea of beauty, of oneness with Nature, which animated the Greek consciousness could be united with the consciousness of sin and of isolation, the consciousness of law and duty which played so large a part in the Christian consciousness.

Then, again, there was the question of the reconciliation of the Church and the State. In both Catholic and Protestant countries the idea of dualism between the two still prevailed. The Catholic held that the Church and the State were in themselves wholly separate. He only contended that in the case of a conflict between the two the interests of the Church, since they represented the eternal and the spiritual side of man, should predominate over the State, which represented only the temporal and worldly side. Even here, however, there was a contradiction in practice; for the Church, as a matter of fact, had become an immense state with widespread temporal and political interests. On the other hand, the Protestants, while confessing in general that the spiritual interests of man were higher than his temporal, still insisted that the State should never be interfered with by the Church. Protestantism held that there could be a division by giving the domain of the internal, the domain of conscience in the sense of subjective ideas and beliefs, wholly to the Church, to religion, while the outward forms of life and the actual points of contact between men should be reserved wholly for the State. But here also there was a confusion. In practice such separation meant that all the final deciding weight should be given to the State as the objective element. At least to separate the inner from the outer was to deprive the internal side of all concrete bases and ends, reducing it to an empty spirituality, while it made the outer side lifeless, perfunctory and without any deep spiritual meaning.

Then there was, finally, the question of how the idea of freedom, individuality, the principle, that is, of the Enlightenment, could be reconciled with the substantial value of history and of social relations. The principle of the Enlightenment in working itself out had apparently resulted in an almost anarchic individualism. Seemingly all social ties, all objective institutions, all settled authority, had been dissolved in favor of an unstable liberty of the individual. The excess of the French Revolution seems to be the logical outcome of the principle of freedom. And yet this conception of individuality, of the rights of the individual, is the animating spring of the whole modern consciousness. Was there no way of uniting this principle of individuality, this conception of the rights of private conscience with the principle of stable outward authority?

Second, as to Hegel's method. We have already noted one main trait of this method, namely, that it is based on a conception of thought, not as a subjective faculty, but as the manifestation of the meaning of reality itself. This idea of method was deepened and almost transformed by Hegel's conviction of the important place of opposition, of contradiction and of negation in life. We have already seen that he was led to conceive of three stages in historical development. First, the period of implicit unity when, apparently, all was harmony; when man and Nature and God were at one. Then, secondly, there was the period of negation and of discord, the period when the various elements of the original unity were isolated and set over against each other. In the third period, however, a true reconciliation takes place. It is seen that underlying the discord and opposition there is still a unity, nay, even more, it is seen that the very principle of difference, of negation, is itself an expression and a realization of this unity,—that the period of discord is an element in the process by which the real harmony maintains and extends itself. Hegel simply translated this process of historical development into terms of thought and by it the character of his method, or of what he called dialectic, was fixed. He recognized, that is, three factors in every process of thought.

25 In the technical development and statement of these three processes, Hegel found support in previous philosophers, notably in Kant and Fichte. Fichte, indeed, had distinctly stated that every process of thought has the three stages of thesis, antithesis and synthesis. In the first stage, that of thesis, thought simply lays itself down, simply declares something to be done, without any element of relation whatever involved. In the second period, that of the antithesis, this original unity is broken up into different elements which are set over against each other. In the third stage, that of synthesis, these are reunited into a truer and higher whole. This was the formal side of Hegel's method. The truth which lay below it was that all thinking involved, like the process of reality itself, a union of affirmative and negative, or of universal and particular factors. Hegel never let go of his conception that the negative side of life was not either a mere unreality or something aside of and apart from the positive. It was his idea that the side of opposition, of apparent discord, and even of contradiction, was the moving spring by which the positive first really made itself positive. That which was prior to such negation could not be called in any true sense a positive. It was positive only because it had not as yet been questioned. Then came the period of apparent negation, the period of denial, of separation. But this, again, was not ultimate; it rested upon a positive; it was only the negation of a positive and therefore, in its complete development, it must give rise to a higher positive. Being negative, it must destroy itself. This third stage Hegel called negation of negations, which, however, is not mere annihilation, but the statement of a positive in which all contradictions had been reconciled.

26 Thus it is that Hegel says that truth is the union of contradictories. Every truth, that is, is a synthesis of two elements, which if isolated would contradict each other, but which, because they do contradict each other in their separation, demand a third higher truth into which each is absorbed. Another way of looking at it is to call the first period one of dogmatic thought, a thought which is not at all aware of its own conditions, limitations and relations. The second period is skepticism, in which all conditions latent in the dogmatic view are

worked out and opposed to each other. For the time being it seems as if all truth had been destroyed and as if doubt were the final word. In reality, however, this doubt is only a doubt of *dogmatic* truth, of truth which does not realize its own basis and bearings. The results, therefore, of a skeptical period must be the discovery of a truth which is aware of its own conditions and relations. This is the period of criticism, that is, of self-conscious thought.

All Hegel's philosophy will be found to run in threes. It may often occur in special instances that these sets of threes are forced and arbitrary, but the principle that lies below them all should be remembered. This is the principle that it is of the very nature of reality, of life and of spirit, to oppose itself and through this opposition to reach its own realized development. First, life, mere life, natural life; and then the death to life, the destruction of the merely natural life; and then, thirdly, through this negation a higher life, a life of the spirit. This is the principle which underlies all of Hegel's triadic divisions.

His philosophy as a whole, for example, is divided into three parts. First, logic; second, philosophy of nature; and, third, philosophy of spirit. Logic is the theory of the implicit or undeveloped spirit, spirit in which the opposition of the subject and the object, of consciousness and of nature, of the ego and non-ego, has not as yet shown itself. Then we have the philosophy of nature which is spirit in its extreme externality, thought which has gone forth out of itself and lost all consciousness of its own spiritual and rational nature. But nature itself gradually gives rise to life, and then to sentient life, life which feels itself. Thus the externality of Nature returns to the internality of Spirit. We get the conscious life of spirit in which the subjective and objective are again united, not as they were at first in the logic, but in a constant process of life. In the logic they were united simply because they had not been separated. In the process of separating, the subjective and the objective, nature and thought, the ego and the non-ego, are each given their due rights in relation to the other. Then opposition is constantly overcome in the very life of the spirit itself.

29. Third, as to his philosophic *antecedents*. We have already noted that Hegel's original impulse was not from the study of philosophy as such, but none the less he was engaged in the study of philosophy, at least all the time after he left the University. At first it was Rousseau, then Kant, then Fichte; later he was in close contact with Schelling himself; and in his Frankfurt period he seems to have studied Plato and the Middle Age mystics. He thus began with the great prophet of the modern idea of liberty and individuality. It was the whole tendency of Rousseau to exalt the individual as absolute, to make the duties of the family, of the civil society and of the state, to make the institutions of science and of art and the whole process of history,—as nothing when compared with the value of the individual to himself. Yet this very process of exalting the individual had been at the expense of isolating him. The higher the individual was declared to be, the more he was cut off from all specific relations in life, and the more empty and thus apparently worthless he became. The individual in himself, the individual to the exclusion of all external and outward relations was declared to be the ultimate principle in life! And yet in this isolated individual what is there which has any value at all? This was the contradiction inherent in the philosophy of the Enlightenment.

30. This problem of later philosophy came to be this: how, without giving up the conception of the individual, of the ego, of the subject as the ultimate and absolute principle,—could some definite content be found within this individual. If all external relations have been cut off and yet the ego is to retain any value, it must be because within the ego the same relations can be found, only transformed and spiritualized by being made free. It is practically at this point that Kant stands. The fundamental principle of his philosophy is what he calls the unity of self-consciousness or the transcendental ego. Back of the individual self, back of nature and the whole process of experience, lies, according to Kant, a unity of self which binds together all things in space and time into one harmonious whole. In spite of the extreme technicality of Kant's philosophy, his system, after all, is nothing but the reflective theory of the modern consciousness, and its end is to

give the real basis and justification of the modern faith in individuality and freedom. Kant, however, left as great a problem as he had solved. What was the relation of this universal ego to the individual ego and the concrete world with its forms of science, art and society? Kant's own position left the two necessarily related, indeed, and yet necessarily opposed. The unity of the self had no meaning nor value excepting as it connected the various elements of the empirical world, and yet by the very necessity of the case this universal ego must always set itself over against the process of experience. On the other hand, this process of experience could never become an adequate manifestation of the unity of the self.

Fichte attempted to solve Kant's problem as follows: The universal spirit can realize itself only on condition that it may have some material against which it acts. It can really act only as it overcomes resistance. This universal ego, therefore, creates the world of sense and of nature in order that it may have something to overcome. It produces it simply for the purpose or sake of getting a stimulus for its own higher action. The ego can realize itself morally only in its struggle with, and conquest of, the world of sense. As a necessary condition, then, of its own moral activity, it must set over against itself the world of experience. But this world of experience has no subsistent reality; it exists only to be destroyed. All forms of necessity are simply stuff by which freedom may be realized.

Now, it is obvious that such a view both involves a contradiction and makes the process of nature and of experience purely subjective. It involves a contradiction, for, if the universal ego should once succeed in overcoming the material which it makes external to itself, that is, if it should succeed in realizing its own activity,—it would destroy itself. Having no more stimulus nor material of action, it would cease to be. Fichte's philosophy, then, leaves us at the point of tension between what we may call the universal principle of the world and the world itself. The universal spirit *is*, not in any true sense, but yet is something which eternally should be. It is, as it were, perpetually perpetrating an illusion upon itself. It creates a world external to itself for the sake of destroying it, and yet it knows that it must not really destroy the outer world, for if it should do that it would also destroy itself. Such a view is also subjective. It gives the realm of Nature and of history no true objective worth. They exist simply for the sake of—merely as a means to—the subjective activity of the ego. Schelling was impelled by these defects to give the problem a new form and a new solution. His idea was that there were two parallel systems of reality. There was Nature, on the one hand, which was a system of objective thought forms, a nature which in itself and for its own sake was a real and true expression of the universal ego. Corresponding to this world of nature was a world of mind which was equally and in like manner an embodiment of the universal ego. Below and back of these two parallel systems was the universal ego itself, the principle of identity in which all opposition of the objective and the subjective was swallowed up.

Now, Hegel for a time, in outward seeming at least, agreed with Schelling's point of view. After leaving Frankfurt he went to Jena and for three years was closely associated with Schelling. They were indeed joint editors of a philosophical journal.[10] The point in which Schelling and Hegel were agreed was, of course, the existence of a unity underlying the opposition between man and nature, between the objective and subjective worlds. This principle of unity they agreed in regarding as absolute spirit or God. They agreed further in holding that this absolute principle manifested itself as truly in the objective world of nature as in the subjective realm of moral action, thus disagreeing with Fichte, who admitted the former as a mere means to the latter. But, from what has been said of Hegel's mode of treatment, it is evident that a deep antagonism existed, latently at least, between his theory and that of Schelling. The unity of Schelling seemed to be an identity undifferentiated in itself, an identity lying back of or underneath opposition. Hegel already at this time had begun to conceive of the unity as not a mere underlying point of union, or as a common substratum, but as a unity of *activity* to be realized in and through diversity and opposition. Schelling's identity seemed to be in itself a mere blank and undifferentiated unity out of which somehow two different yet corresponding worlds arose. This absolute identity, then, which to Schelling was the highest principle of all philosophy, could be to Hegel only a starting point. It was simply the implicit unity, the reality which had not as yet gone forth and manifested itself. The true absolute could be found only when this original identity had differentiated itself and when out of its differences it had reached a unity of life and of activity in which the subject and the object no longer expressed two parallel lines, but were themselves factors contributing to the higher unity of the spirit.

This original defect of Schelling's also led, in Hegel's mind, to another defect. Not perceiving that all difference is the first step in the unfolding of the great spiritual reality which comprehends all things, Schelling really had no method by which he could trace the various phases either of thought or of the world. Schelling thus fell back on what he called intellectual intuition, a sort of direct perception of the original identity and of corresponding forms of mind and nature which grew out of it.

Hegel's elements of opposition to Schelling soon became overt and in the preface of his first published philosophical work, the *Phenomenology of Spirit*,[11] Hegel breaks once for all with the standpoint and method of Schelling. Among other things in his preface Hegel says that the identity of Schelling is simply like the blackness[12] of night in which all cows are black. Again, he says that Schelling's identity is like a lion's den into which all the tracks of thought lead, but out of which none proceed. Again, he says that the results of Schelling are obtained as if they were shot out of a pistol. The essence of philosophy, he says, is to comprehend absolute truth, not simply as substance but as subject. All these various sayings point in one direction. They are modes of saying that Schelling's principle is too immediate; that it lacks the factor of development. Schelling had made the absolute simply an identity in which differences of subject and object, man and nature, were swallowed up. This is what Hegel means by substance. By subject, on the other hand, Hegel understands a spiritual principle which maintains itself as unity, not by abolishing distinctions, but by making them elements in its own self-conscious life. It is a principle of activity as against one of mere existence. As regards, then, the relation of nature and mind Hegel may be said to unite Fichte and Schelling. Like Fichte, he holds that the world of nature is not of equal value with the life of spirit; he denies, that is, that mind and nature are simply two parallel systems of equal value set over against each other. But at the same time, he agrees with Schelling in holding that nature is not a mere obstacle to be overcome by spirit. It is itself the real and true manifestation of spirit. He reconciles the two, then, by conceiving of spirit as an active unity in which all absolute oppositions are overcome but in which they are maintained as relative distinctions. Nature, for example, is neither swallowed up in spirit nor of equal value with it. It is a factor in the process of spirit itself and spirit maintains itself by means of the eternal maintaining of nature in existence.

36 It should never be forgotten amid all the technicalities and details of Hegel's statement that he has not abandoned his original problem. The idea of a universal ego, of spirit as itself found in Hegel's philosophy, is simply a theoretical formulation of the idea of subjectivity, of individuality, of freedom, which has played so large a part in the modern consciousness. How are we to justify the large claims which are made for the individual both in political and intellectual matters? Only by seeing that the individual is more than a mere individual, that he is not a being by himself exclusive of all objective relationships, but that in his true nature he is a focus in which all these objective relations come to conscious unity. By such a conception of the individual Hegel overcame the weakness of the Enlightenment while he retained its strength. Its weakness had been its inability to reconcile the principle of individual freedom with the substantial reality manifested in the objective world and in society. In the process of knowledge, for example, in order to save the subjective side of it, it was necessary either wholly to deny the existence of the objective world, reducing it to mere clusters of sensations found in the individual mind itself; or to treat it as a mere unknown cause lying back of experience, experience itself being wholly individual and subjective in character. So, on the side of practice, in order to save its principle of individual freedom from external dogmatic authority and control, it

was obliged to reduce the moral life to a mere succession of feelings whose end was happiness in the sense of an aggregate of particular pleasures. Having no way of reconciling the objective constitution of the State with this principle of individual freedom, it turned upon the former and declared that law and government were by their nature limitations upon freedom and hence, at the most, were to be endured as necessary evils.

Hegel, by his conception of subjectivity or spirit as the ultimate reality of the world, was able to reach the standpoint from which he could give objective value to nature and to the State without thereby making them external burdens upon man's own activity or limits of his freedom. Nature and the State are both forms in which spirit realizes itself. The individual as he is born into the world of physical and social relations may at first find these external and hostile to him, but, as the spiritual principle latent within him develops, it finds that these two relations are after all akin to itself, and it is only as the subjective spirit takes for its own and makes a part of itself these objective relations that it becomes spiritual or free in any real sense. Hegel, that is, saves the principle by showing that individuality includes, rather than excludes, concrete relations of Nature and of the State; but includes them not in any passive way but in and through its activity. In order to be itself the spirit has to master the realm of its outward relations, and in mastering them truly masters itself and thus makes itself free. The whole question of modern life is precisely how are we to reconcile the principle of the spiritual with the concrete values of our actual life, without at the same time falling a prey to external authority or to merely internal sentiments. Hegel solves the problem by declaring that the individual is himself an expression of the absolute spirit, that in order to realize this unity with the absolute spirit in which consists his freedom, he has to work himself out in the definite forms of science, art, religion and state.

1. Hegel begins his Philosophy of Spirit with the declaration that it is simply the fulfillment of the historic command to man to "Know thyself." For man to know himself belongs to the very nature of spirit. The command to knowledge of self is not a law imposed on the spirit

by some foreign power. The God which impels man to self-knowledge is none other than the spirit's own absolute law. All activity of spirit is just this self-knowledge, and the nature of all true science is only that the spirit shall know itself in everything which is in Heaven and upon earth. Anything that is entirely foreign to the spirit does not exist. Even the Oriental did not wholly lose himself in the object of his adoration. The Greeks recognized that which they worshiped as divine as somehow akin to themselves. But in Christianity man recognizes the true infinity of his own spirit and therefore for the first time becomes truly free. The philosophy of spirit is simply the knowledge of the process by which the spirit works out its true infinity.

39   2. Hegel distinguishes his philosophy of spirit in its standpoint and method from both empirical and rational psychology. Rational psychology regards the soul as a sort of thing, as a simple substance, immaterial, an essence behind all phenomena, and as static and rigid. But spirit is absolute unrest, it is active, it is not merely simple, but a unity whose very nature is to express itself in definite and specific forms. It is not a ready-made substance keeping itself to itself behind the mass of phenomena, but is actual only in and through definite modes of its necessary self-revelation; only in and through phenomena, that is to say. It is not a thing in some external relation to the body, but exists in organic unity with it.

40   While rational psychology sets up a ready-made and abstract soul, empirical psychology begins with a lot of ready-made faculties, not attempting to show any necessary connection between these faculties and the nature of spirit itself. It resolves the soul into an aggregate of independent powers which stand in mechanical relations to each other. The philosophy of spirit shows that these so-called faculties of mind, and also all concrete empirical material, are simply elements in the development of the active unity of spirit. We understand spirit, then, not when we begin by supposing a substance which we term soul or by supposing a lot of separate mental faculties, but only when we trace the varied process by which spirit realizes itself. Our so-called faculties will then appear in their proper place as stages in

its evolution. Thus the whole science becomes living, organic and systematic.

3. What, then, does Hegel mean by spirit? Nature, he says, is the presupposition, the basis of spirit, and spirit is the negation of nature. What are we to understand by this somewhat Delphic sounding statement? Hegel says that if we ask what nature is, it is indeed rational, the manifestation of thought, but of thought in the form of externality. Everything material is external to the mind; indeed, the material is external to itself. It exists spread out endlessly in space and time, and it is the very nature of every atom of it to repel every other atom. In the animal organism this externality of nature is somewhat overcome. Each member of the animal body is cause and effect of every other: each organ is at once means and ends of every other. All the parts are so penetrated (permeated) by the unity of the whole that nothing which happens in the whole is external or indifferent to it. Sensation is just this unity of the organism throughout all its members. In sensation any specific sensation made on any particular part is at once felt by the whole, and as an affection of the whole. At first, the particular impression is wholly lost in the unity of the organic sensation, but the sensation produces a craving, a need. It arouses impulses. Thus the animal is aroused out of its mere unity and set in opposition to its surroundings. The appetite, however, leads the animal to attack something in its surroundings to satisfy itself. Thus its unity is restored.

We have here a sort of symbol or foreshadowing of the process of spirit. In sensation, in feeling, the soul is at one with the object. But when self-consciousness rises this unity breaks into two, the object is set over against the subject, the subject against the object. But this division makes a contradiction in spirit, whose very nature is to be an active unity. The subject, therefore, sets to work to subdue the object to itself. The difference in the process as it takes place in the mere animal and in man is that in the animal the process is not self-conscious. The animal never consciously recognizes its own nature and never makes it objective to itself, and thus it never has a world of known objects: it never has reason, intelligence in the true sense.

The animal consciousness, again, does not recognize its own unity, it does not set up this unity as an end or an ideal to be secured and maintained. Thus it never has a world of objective aims to realize; it has no true will. Spirit, then, as distinct from mere feeling organism, frees itself from nature by making its own being self-conscious. Having thus set nature over against itself, it then, as it were, turns around and proceeds by knowledge, art and conduct, to transform this outer nature into a factor of its own activity.

43 This process is what Hegel means by nature being the basis of spirit and spirit being the negative of Nature. All the activities of spirit, says Hegel, are only ways by which the external is brought back to the internal, is made ideal. Only through this process of restoration, through this idealizing or assimilating of the external, does the spirit come to be. This negative power of spirit, its power to make abstraction of all particular content and still to be itself, constitutes the ego, the I. Taken as merely negative, this ego is a bare or abstract universal. It is the I am I which sets itself up to the exclusion of things in space and time and of all other persons. But the ego, thus recognizing its universality, is an active negative, it is not bare emptiness. It therefore attacks all the material set over against it. It makes this material its own and thus stamps upon it its own universality. In the same way the ego loses its isolated universality and becomes a definite spiritual being. The spirit does not lose itself in the manifold material which it deals with, but weaves together many threads into a unity of its own life. Spirit, so far, however, is still finite. It has an external world over against it and simply works against it, gradually overcoming and transmuting it. But in religion and philosophy the shell of externality is entirely broken through. The spirit of man penetrates the spirit of which nature and history are only expressions. It thus no longer struggles to conquer what is external to itself, but realizes that this apparent externality is in truth of one spirit with itself. In the complete union of the subjective spirit, the ego or personality of man and the objective spirit as manifested in nature and in society is found the absolute spirit.

In philosophy which deals with absolute spirit, Hegel says, man is not dealing with a material external to himself. Just as every great historic character is at once made by his times but in turn makes his times, so with philosophic knowledge, it is at once the expression, the content of reality, and at the source of truth. Just as the historic character, in other words, simply elevates time to complete consciousness so that what he does is simply the complete energy of his times come to a focus and thereby transforming itself, so with philosophic energy. It is not the process by which the individual mind knows a reality over against itself, it is the process by which this reality comes to a consciousness of its own basis, meaning and bearings.

The spirit's relation to nature, however, is not to be understood as if nature were the first thing, as if that were the original power. Nature is rather dependent upon spirit, and spirit is the absolute beginning. The appearance with which we begin, namely, that spirit is dependent upon something external, as upon nature, is destroyed by spirit itself, as it works itself out. Spirit has the supreme ingratitude to reduce that upon which it seems to be dependent to a dependent element of itself. It makes it something which is formed and fixed by its own activity. In this way the spirit makes itself perfectly independent; that is to say, the transition from nature to spirit is not a transition to something else, it is only that of the spirit which has been, as it were, lost in nature.

Two other essential characteristics of the spirit are its freedom and its self-revealing power. The very essence of spirit is freedom; that is what we mean when we say that spirit is the ideality, the negativity of Nature. Spirit can set itself over against everything that is outside of it and in this opposition to everything else, it can still retain and assert its own being. It can even bear the negation of its own individual character; that is to say, it can bear an infinite self-negation or pain. So, too, evil is nothing which comes upon the spirit from without, it is only the spirit itself placing itself upon the very summit of its independence. While natural things cannot endure resistance or contradiction, since they pass away when they are negated, spirit can sustain itself even under infinite self-denial. This power of the spirit over all particular and special relations, its power to get along with them, its power to endure when they are taken away or even when they oppose it, is its universality, its freedom. This, however, is only an abstract freedom, it is the freedom of the spirit "by itself," that is potentially unrealized. Spirit attains to positive freedom, not when it withdraws from all positive relations and still maintains its identity, but only when it impresses its own identity upon all the material which seems to resist it. Freedom, that is to say, does not remain a mere power of spirit, but the spirit gains freedom as it gains actual power, and it gains this actual power just in the degree in which it transmutes all things into tools of its own action.

47   The very nature of the spirit is to manifest, to reveal itself. This does not mean that spirit reveals *something,* that it makes something known. We are accustomed to think of revelation as an empty form which may reveal this thing or that thing or the other as it happens. In the ordinary conception there is no intrinsic relation between the process of relation and its content, that which is revealed. But the spirit reveals precisely itself; the revelation and the revealed are the same thing. In other words, the outward form which the spirit gives itself is the absolute, transparent expression of its own inner nature. Taken simply on its inner side, as the revealer without the revelation, spirit would be only a potentiality. It exists only as it manifests itself, only as this potentiality becomes actual.

48   Spirit is, then, the absolute, and the absolute the spirit. This means just this,—that spirit is the one complete and independent activity, not independent in the sense that it gets along without things, but independent in the sense that it succeeds in reducing all things to factors, to instruments of its own action, indeed, in the sense that in final analysis, these very things which the spirit uses in order to realize itself are only its own objective manifestation.

49   Self-revelation has three distinct forms. In the first place, thought externalizes itself in nature. Secondly, thought returns to itself through and by means of this externality. It becomes self-conscious, and, in the finite spirit, idealizes nature and reduces it to a oneness

with itself. But nature is still a limit to spirit. It is something other than spirit which spirit has to master in order to really be. So the third and highest revelation of spirit is that in which the dualism of an independent nature, on one side, and of spirit on the other, which is transforming nature into itself, has vanished. The absolute spirit is that which reveals itself both in nature and in the finite spirit. Nature is no longer a limit which has to be overcome by spirit, but simply a stage in the process by which self-consciousness elevates itself to its own complete and objective being.

The whole philosophy of spirit is divided into three parts. First, the Subjective; second, the Objective; and third, the Absolute Spirit, the subjective and the objective being included under the head of finite. The subjective spirit is spirit in its process of coming to self-consciousness, spirit as it is withdrawing out of its slavery to nature and becoming aware of its own universal character. It is called subjective for the very reason that it implies this withdrawal from nature. It is free by itself only; it is not free objectively or outwardly. It is what we ordinarily mean by the I, when we emphasize the conscious individual, I, as aware of itself as against all objects and as against all other persons. But the spirit is not content with this inner freedom and universality. It must seek, as we have already said, objectively to realize its freedom. Thus it brings forth, as it were, a new world; it utilizes the material of nature by forming out of it ends and ideals and then proceeding to realize these ends. It does not simply draw itself up in proud self-consciousness, and say that I am I, higher than every thing material, but it tries to put this I out into the world to make the world conformable[13] to its own spirit nature, to make the things simply tools of its own power. This, of course, is illustrated in the process of industry and applied science. It reaches its summit in the State, where the inner freedom of man becomes outward in a whole organized system of laws and institutions. The world of history is at once a world produced by man and a world objective to man. It is, that is to say, man himself as he gets objective expression, as he gets out of his mere self-consciousness and realizes the actual ends and relations, at first only implicit in himself. The absolute spirit is the spirit which does not have to overcome an external material, but which is thoroughly conscious of itself in and through all material. In every thing which seems most foreign to it, it still finds its own presence and its own activity. This absolute spirit is manifested in art, religion and philosophy.

Beginning now with the subjective spirit, that is, subdivided into three heads: Anthropology, Phenomenology and Psychology. In anthropology, the spirit is treated as it still stands in closest contact with nature, climate, soil, physical surroundings, conditions of sex and of all the circumstances and vicissitudes of physical life. The spirit in this direct contact with nature, hardly as yet rising out of nature, Hegel calls the soul, the natural spirit, but in this science of anthropology itself the soul gradually rises above nature. It does not indeed escape from the body, but subordinates the body into an outward sign and into a tool, into a representation of the self. The phenomenology considers the soul in its process of rising to practical self-consciousness. It begins with man's consciousness as such, with the ego, the I in its abstractness, in its empty freedom. It is the spirit as standing in relation to nature and in negative relation to it, but not having as yet realized what it means to be I, to be conscious. All concrete content seems external to the I. The activity of the I consists in this, then, to fill up the void of its abstract selfness, to take the objective over into itself and to make the merely subjective, objective. The result of this process is that man comes to self-consciousness, to what we may term reason. Psychology takes the soul at this point. Spirit and reason stand to each other in the same relation as body and weight, as will and freedom. Reason forms the substantial nature of spirit. Thus reason grasping itself on the subjective side is intelligence; on the objective side, it is practical reason or will.

Intelligence, at first without any content, destroys its own inadequate form when it takes the material which stands over against it, the material which exists as[14] bare brute particular facts and by measuring them according to the absolute standard of reason gives them a certain rationality. This translates them into a universal form more like itself. In this process of intelligence, reason comes to the consciousness of its own powers of generalization, and in this way it becomes will. Will is intelligence dealing, not with external particulars, but with internal particulars; with appetites, inclinations, etc. Just as intelligence, as theoretical reason translates the objective particulars into[15] the universal form, so the will, as pure reason, gives the subjective particulars a universal form. It changes them into universals[16] It takes the mere inclination out of its mere isolation and organizes it into unity with all the aims and ends of life.

We begin, then, with Anthropology whose object is the soul. We must bear in mind here that by the soul Hegel does not mean any particular soul, nor individual consciousness. He does not mean, indeed, that there is any soul in general apart from individual souls, but simply that we have not yet arrived at the point where we can deal with souls individualized as the ego. What he means, then, by soul, is the whole process of nature itself, so far as that has become internal to itself, so far as that has been transformed into a feeling of itself. We may, perhaps, understand what Hegel means if we take the process of evolution to the exclusion of all particular forms which are evolved. We cannot think of this or that particular individual, but we can think of the process of evolution itself out of which every species of individual comes, and back into which it goes.

Suppose we take this process of evolution simply with reference to the development of human beings. From one point of view, we can regard all these different human beings simply as so many accidents or qualities into which the one substantial process of life has differentiated itself during its evolution. The individual is thus regarded as so many waves which the sea causes to rise out of its own substance, and which it finally causes to fall into its own substance. That is to say, we may take the common substratum of consciousness itself which underlies all particularized consciousness and will. We speak in this way of the soul of man, meaning by it neither the soul of any particular man nor aggregate of men, but a sort of substratum which lies behind all the special individual persons. Now if we take the soul of man in its generic sense and think of it especially in its connections with the world of nature, we have something like what Hegel means by the soul as the object of anthropology. Anthropology has for its subject matter, then, this single developing soul of man, considered not with reference to its spiritual achievements but simply with reference to its own contact with nature.

55 Hegel thus says that the standpoint of the soul, if we do not get beyond it, lies at the basis of philosophical pantheism. All the Oriental religions and philosophies are essentially pantheistic. They conceive of the reality of things as a sort of vast single soul which gives birth to, and in turn destroys all particular objects and all persons. The soul is neither matter nor self-conscious spirit; it is a sort of direct unity in which the material and the spiritual are one.

56 In strong opposition to this ancient view is the modern one which sets the soul over against nature. It makes a thing out of matter and another thing out of the soul and then asks how it is possible that these two fixed and separate things should have any relation to each other. The question put is, by its very nature, insoluble, and thus we have from the persons who put this problem long dissertations upon the incomprehensibility, upon the mysteriousness of the relations of the soul to matter. The true solution is found when the problem is stated in its true terms. Matter is not one thing and soul another; it is the very nature of matter to come to itself out of its externality, and thus to feel itself, to become internal and ideal. Matter, in other words, is so far from being the fixed, rigid opposition of soul that it must necessarily in its development manifest itself as soul. The soul, in other words, is the truth of matter; it is the real meaning of matter. We may see that this is so, if we take the standpoint of materialism. Once admit that matter is the sole existence, that all feeling and all thought are the outcome of matter; what is this but saying that matter in the highest forms of its activity and organization manifests itself as feeling and as thought.

57 Take, for example, Tyndall's statement that we may see in matter the promise and the potency of all conscious life. At first sight, this seems to reduce consciousness to the plane of matter. This is so if we look at it from the beginning, from the first end, but if we look at it from the side of the process by which it is best revealed in its

outcome, it is simply to say that matter is spirit in its potentiality, that we have spirit all the time. Only undeveloped spirit is what we call matter; it is spirit external to itself. In other words, it makes no practical difference in the outcome whether we take the standpoint of materialism or idealism providing only we will be consistent with ourselves and look at every thing from the standpoint of this one principle. As Hegel says, in ordinary materialism it is entirely overlooked that the cause goes into its effect. In other words, we get the satisfactory meaning and value of the cause only when we know the effect. We know what the means are only when we see the end which they bring about. To say thus that matter is the cause of soul is to say simply that it is the very nature of matter to become soul, that the soul is the real meaning, the real truth of matter, and this is precisely what is meant by idealism. It is only when we assume an original idealism, a hard and fixed separation of mind and matter, that we cannot[17] avoid dualism, and this dualism practically refutes itself by confessing that the outcome of its own premises is something truly mysterious.

We begin, then, in anthropology, with the soul, with nature still clinging to it, still determining it. The soul has not risen to that point of consciousness of self where it can say that I am I. It simply exists, and in its existence it takes up into itself all the necessities of nature. This soul, Hegel says, is sleeping spirit. He begins by considering the soul as it is affected by climate, by the influences of night and day and of the seasons. Astrology illustrates the same point. It is not, of course, true that the stars affect man's life, but the fact that people once thought they did is at least a sign of a period in which the soul of man and natural influences were thought to be in the most direct connection with each other. Hegel in this portion of his treatise makes the fullest allowance for the determining influence which the physical surroundings can have upon the human soul. He only differs from Buckle and Draper, who have attempted to trace back all historic events to the influences of this environment in this respect. Buckle and Draper make these surroundings the cause of the conscious states and events. Hegel treats them rather as *factors* in the conscious state. They simply translate themselves into consciousness, giving it its basis, its substratum. More than this, Hegel holds that *out* of this substratum the principle of subjectivity, of the ego, finally develops, and that this can use its own substratum, its natural sides, as a tool for its own ends. The soul, as affected by all these phases of nature, is to Hegel simply the material which in time grows into the higher and freer life.

After treating of these physical concerns, Hegel goes on to treat the soul as differentiated into what we may call the different race souls. He discusses the various racial peculiarities at some extent and attempts to show that they mark certain phases of the relation of the soul to nature. The racial soul then differentiates itself still further; there are nationalities, there are what we may term the local or provisional spirits. Nature determines the external way of living, the occupation of the race, and this in turn shapes the inner tendency and capacity of the peoples' character. Thus we have a fishing people, whose occupation is fixed originally by surroundings, but in turn this occupation gives rise to the peculiar emotional and mental traits of the people. We have here what is generally called a spirit of nationality, that spirit which runs through all different individuals of the same nationality and gives them a certain indescribable unity of feeling and attitude.

Hegel illustrates this development in all great historic nationalities. We may take as an example of his mode of treatment what he says about the French, English and German. The French, he says, show both fixity of thought and mobility of wit or emotion. They are a people who delight in general views, in abstract principles; who carry out their general principles in detail regardless of particular consequences. This same fixity and firmness of their understanding gives them a great taste for clearness and definiteness, both of thought and expression. They dislike mystery. But this very attitude of mind is necessarily very one-sided. The logical understanding is abstract, picking out now this side of the thing, now that, and so the French, in feeling out their ideas, fail to get the whole out of life. An illustration is the time of the Revolution and immediately afterward, when all factors of political thought were carried out, not in their union, but separately, one after the other.

The English are a people of the particular rather than the general. They do not care much for the rational in the form of generalities. Their poets, therefore, stand higher than their philosophers. They do not[18] put much stress upon generality, but on[19] the independence of persons. The individual is to be a center in himself. On account of this disregard of general principles, law and rights in England are not derived from general principles but are established by precedent, historic accident. They take the form rather of established detail than of recognized principle. With this love of detail comes the Englishman's practical activity, his commercial spirit.

The Germans are deep, but often unclear in their theories. They want to get at the innermost nature and connection of things. Their spirit is turned within more than that of any European nation. They cannot act until they have thought the principles of their action. The result of these two traits is often a formalism on the part of thought and a failure to act properly. Since they will not act without reasons, the occasion for acting often goes by while they are hunting for a reason. When they have been pressed in their political life, they have often contented themselves with drawing formal statements and protests rather than to act. Although their political spirit is not very vital, they have always had an extraordinary sense of honor, of position, and have been rather of the opinion that the office and the title made the man.

When still further particularized, this natural soul occasions what we call temperament, original capacity, tastes and natural disposition. Each of these points Hegel discusses at some length. So far we have been considering the soul on its static side, in the various outward forms in which it manifests itself. If we take it on its active side, we get another series of distinctions. For example, there are the various stages of life from infancy to old age; there are the sexual relations; the opposition of waking and sleeping in life, etc.

This stage of the development of the soul comes about as follows: So far Hegel has traced the relations by which the natural soul, in itself universal, is particularized or given more definite form in the race, national and local spirit, and then still further in the genius and disposition of the individual soul. These characteristics are considered as fastened upon the soul from without; they are fixed distinctions. But now the soul has gained a certain individuality. Its qualities are not so much thrust upon it from without as changes which it undergoes in itself. The process of the law of these changes is as follows:—The particular soul is, as it were, an accident, a mere particular manifestation of the universal soul which is the substance. But now this accident, this attribute, has to work out its relations. The individual soul, in other words, with its peculiar characteristics of occupation, surroundings, nationality and race, has to elevate itself to the plane of the world's soul. It has to get out of its mere particular existence and realize within itself the generic soul of which it is one differentiation. The individual soul seems to be set over against his kind, his genus,[20] and the latter seems to possess all the real power and substance. Of course the full attainment of the individual to his substantial or generic being can be found only in self-conscious life. Here, where the soul has not yet become conscious of itself as distinct from nature, we can only trace the series of changes which the soul goes through on account of the presence of the generic soul in it.

65   First we have the changes which constitute the life growth of the soul. In infancy the soul is merely subjective and over against it there is merely objective world. The soul is potential for it is undeveloped. The world is only potential, it is not a world to the child, but only stuff, material, for a world. The development is the process by which the soul gets out of its merely subjective condition. The man recognizes the objective necessity and rationality of the world and at the same time makes himself amount to something in it. He gets a definite place and function in the objective world. The relation of sex is another form in which the individual comes to consciousness of a generic or universal nature, largely indeed within his particular existence, and yet constituting his true nature.

66   As the soul gets more reality it gets to an active condition, that of being awake. In sleep the soul is at one with its surroundings. The

awakened soul is interested, it sets itself against its surroundings, not however, absolutely, but in such a way that it directs itself to these surroundings, it attends to them. It is in a constant condition of stretching out. The realization of the individual soul, of the generic soul, of the universal ideality of nature, is brought about mainly in sensation. In sensation the universal character of the soul manifests itself. The soul manifests itself against every outward impression, and translates these outward impressions into their own inner condition. Sensation, in other words, is the universal in the particular. This is at once its strength and the weakness of feeling. Every feeling is a particular condition of the soul and yet the whole soul is in that particular condition. The soul does not regard the feeling as something external and indefinite to itself, but it identifies this whole being absolutely with the feeling. On this account everything in the higher conscious life must grow out of sensation, out of feeling; science, art, religion, all are in feeling. This is because this feeling is the first expression of the soul's own nature, it is the identification of itself with the content, and to say that art, science, etc., grow out of feeling is simply to say that they have come, not from any external source, but from the soul itself. When, however, it is said that sensation is the origin of these higher powers, it only means that sensation is undeveloped science, or art, for by the word origin we mean nothing but the first, most direct way, and therefore most rudimentary way in which a thing manifests itself.

The soul, then, feels itself in all its sensations and hence the absolute certainty of sensation. A person cannot doubt pain or light or sound. They are the one absolutely immediate certain thing: they are certain because the soul is absolutely one with them. They are not set over against the being of the soul at all, and hence there is no chance for doubt or questioning to come in. For the soul to doubt what it felt would be for it to doubt itself, its feelings. But the weakness of sensation, its particular transitory and shifting character, has its ground here also. Certain as is the sensation, it is only the fact of its occurrence that is certain. What is felt, the content of sensation, is absolutely uncertain. Just because the soul is immediately and directly at one with its own sensation, because it has not defined itself, the sensation is vague and changing. The soul that argues from its feelings to truth always confounds the form and the substance. Really we only know that we have felt something, but we make a mantle of this general certainty to spread itself over any doctrine or idea which has come in contact with it, however sporadic and accidental this contact may be.

68   People are directly certain only of what they have not defined; they confuse their self-certainty with the certainty of the particular doctrine in question, simply for the reason that they have not defined their feeling, they have not set it over against themselves. Thus is it that people who argue about politics and religion get angry so easily. They are certain there is some truth in what they say because there is something there by which they have absolutely identified themselves. But the certainty which comes from this feeling of themselves they identify with the certainty of the subject matter, and thus when the subject matter is attacked they feel as if they themselves were attacked in the most sacred and most certain parts of their being. In other words, there is a contradiction in the very nature of sensation. The sensation is the universal directly present in the particular, that is, it is the whole soul directly present in some particular condition of itself. It is, Hegel says, as a universal water could still exist as universal in some colored water. Just because the universal is present in this undefined, unrelated way the sensation must change. The particular is not adequate to express the universal and therefore that the universal may be wholly expressed it gives way to another feeling, etc. Not till the soul has definitely worked out in specific form its own universal nature can its particular expression be other than a changing accidental state.

69   Since the soul is directly one with its particular condition there is in sensation no opposition of subjective and objective. This distinction does not exist consciously or for the soul, but only in the content of the sensations themselves. The sensations themselves, therefore, become divided into two classes, an outer and an inner. The outer sensations are the direct translation of nature into the soul's own

inner life; they are such experiences as light, sound, heat, etc. But we have also the life of the soul itself, the soul in its own true inner nature. And since the soul is still a unity with nature, it can feel its own qualities only so far as these find bodily expression. Just as a man can make others feel his feelings only as he expresses them by some bodily gesture or outward sign, so a man cannot feel his own feelings except as they come in this round-about way through his body. For anything to be felt it must at once be distinguished from the soul, that is, be particularized, and yet identified with the soul, and this distinction and identification takes place through bodily sensation. That is to say, sadness or joy, scorn, hatred, courage, etc., are not felt directly and of themselves; they are felt only through the outward bodily expression. Take away this bodily expression and there is nothing left to characterize the feeling; we have only the blank, undisturbed identity of the soul itself.

Hegel discusses, then, an expression of emotions on this basis, attempting to show how any particular concrete expression of the various emotions symbolizes to the soul its own feelings. Humor, for example, is the consciousness of the nothingness of some object present to the consciousness. It is the consciousness of something which amounts to nothing, something which immediately destroys itself; this trivial thing, this self-destructive thing, not being in any way identified with ourselves. In the experience, then, the comic or the humorous, the subjectivity of the spectator comes to a complete and untroubled enjoyment of itself. This humor is indeed the consciousness of a soul as itself superior to the outward destruction as capable of experiencing it and yet being unaffected by it. Now, with this inner humor the physiological expression is in direct agreement, for in laughing this untroubled subjective enjoyment, the pure self, is like a light which spreads over the whole countenance. The self, having nothing opposed to it, radiates as it were through the entire body. The explosive act of laughter is simply the symbolic expression of the spiritual act by which the soul repels the laughed-at-thing from itself saying, as it were, it is no affair of mine. Speech is the highest form of the expression of the feelings. Speech is the outward token through which the feeling expresses itself. Only in speech, therefore, does the soul truly feel its own feelings. But when it does thus completely realize them, the feelings are so defined that they cease to be feelings, and thus we are taken beyond the scope of anthropology.

71 All particular sensations, as we have said, are transitory because they are not adequate expressions of the universal nature of the soul, although they pretend to be. The true being of the sensation is indeed its passing away. It thus recognizes its failure to be what it claims to be. Over and above, then, all particular sensations we have the soul itself which reduces, one after another, its own feelings to past conditions of itself. These feelings, indeed, do not pass away, they remain simply as modifications of the way in which the soul itself feels. If it were possible for the soul consciously to remember one of these past experiences it would not be the natural soul any more, but would have attained to the conscious soul, the soul which can make its own conditions objective to itself. The past experiences, however, remain simply ideal, latent within the soul itself. Every soul is in this condition so far as it cannot make objective to itself its own experiences or, as we ordinarily express it, so far as it cannot remember its own past.

72 Feeling, by which Hegel means sensation, appetites, impulses and passions, so far as it loses its independence and becomes reduced to a capacity of the soul itself,—is habit. The soul in this way comes to possess its experiences instead of being absorbed in them. It has them in itself, without being obliged to feel them, and it thus moves freely in them. It is free from them so far as it is not interested in them, as it is not constantly taken up with them, and thus is not only left open to other occupations but also has an additional power to bring to bear on this other occupation. Habit, then, is the freedom which the soul obtains over its particular experiences by reducing them into powers of its own. It is the mechanism of feeling by which the particular feelings are reduced to organs of the soul itself.

73 There are three stages in the development of habit: first, being accustomed to sensations and thus reducing them to indifferent things. Thus[21] the soul becomes to heat and cold, to weariness, etc.,—independent. The soul, in other words, is no longer carried away by

every experience. In the second place, the soul becomes indifferent to the satisfaction of its appetites. Through habit the soul is freed from the necessity of immediate and direct satisfaction. In the third place, habit takes the form of skill, active habit, and from the soul makes itself felt through the body and subjects the latter to its own use. Habit is thus the process by which the soul comes to possess itself, to know its experiences instead of being lost in them. That unity of the body and the soul which merely *existed* in feeling is transformed in habit into a *made* unity, a unity which is the outcome of the soul's own activity. It thus forms also the transition between the soul and the whole outer world. It is getting the mastery of the body through habit that the soul gets the power to master the whole world. In other words, mere feeling represents the flooding of the soul by nature; feeling changed into a capacity reverses the movement and enables the soul to project itself into nature. Through this process the soul appropriates the body to itself and the body becomes at once the outward token and the tool of the soul. Speech is the highest evidence of this fact.

The soul which has freed itself from dependence upon particular states, and which has reduced its particular experience to the means of expressing itself, is no longer the mere soul. The universal is no longer one with the particular, but has got a certain preponderance over the particular by getting outside of it. So we have here the transition from soul to consciousness. By consciousness Hegel means that stage of development of spirit in which the self regards the totality of what was formerly its own states as an object or world external to itself. But at the same time it is its own world, a world of which it is as certain as it is of itself. The feelings which were formerly one with the soul are now an object to the soul. The ego, says Hegel, is the lightning which strikes through the natural soul and devours its merely natural aspects.

That part of his philosophy which treats of consciousness as distinct from the soul Hegel calls phenomenology. By consciousness he means the ordinary attitude of the mind toward objects,—when the mind seems to be one thing and the object another thing and yet the sole use of consciousness is to be conscious of objects and the object is always an object of consciousness. It is at this point of consciousness, then, that the great difficulty of modern philosophy arises. How does it come about that the world seems independent of consciousness and external to it while at the same time it can be known only in relation to consciousness, only as its object? The characteristic point in Hegel's treatment of the problem is that he does not isolate this question of the relation of subject and object and consider it by itself: he shows us where it comes from and where it goes to, that is to say, he shows us how, in the development of spirit starting with the soul, that which was first a simple content of the soul becomes transformed into an object, and hence apparently is thrown outside of it. He shows us also that the distinction is not a fixed separation but is one stage in the process of spirit by which it ultimately affects its own particular unity or activity.

76 In the beginning of our study of consciousness we seem to have simply the bare fact of a relation between subject and object. Since we do not know what the relation is, the relation seems to be arbitrary and external. The ego on the one side seems to be purely subjective and the object, on the other, purely objective, that is, external to consciousness. The contradiction is that consciousness is just as certain of the object as it is of itself. The object, in other words, is both in and without consciousness; it is in consciousness simply as known object; it is out of consciousness because the rationality of its content not being understood, it is not seen to be one with consciousness itself. The dialectic here, then, is the process by which the self finds out that the object is identical with spirit and that the apparent independence of the subject is due simply to the self-division of spirit. In this process certainty is elevated to truth. There is no certainty from the start because the ego has the absolute certainty of itself, but only when it finds out its own nature and becomes rationally aware of the identity of objects with itself is this certainty transformed into truth. A child is absolutely certain of every object which it sees but only science can see the object in its truth; see it, that is, in the relations which make it what it is. Certainty is the direct conviction of the fact;

truth is knowledge of the fact in its reason and ground, the knowledge not only that it is so but why it is so. In the history of philosophy, the Scotch philosophy of natural realism illustrates the standpoint of certainty. This conviction simply consists in asserting that we are directly conscious of objects and that nothing can rob us of our conviction that we know objects just as truly as we know ourselves. Kant attempted to transform this certainty into truth, that is, he attempted to show how and why it was that self could have an objective consciousness. Consciousness which has realized its positive relations with the object known is reason.

The first step in the advance toward reason is sense perception. Here the object has no more value for thought than simply to be the object of thought. This minimum of relation to consciousness cannot be got rid of, but since it is a mere empty relation no essential connections between the object and reason are known. The mind has before it an indefinite multitude of separate and independent objects. But as consciousness makes each of these things an object to itself, it finds out that each object has certain relations to others, it finds out that every quality of an object implies relation of other objects. And if you take away this relation, the quality itself vanishes. The quality of color implies a relation to waves of ether, on one side, and to a nervous organism, on the other. Change one of these related objects and the quality changes. Finally the object seems to dissolve into this network of relations. Thus the relations seem to have a certain universality and permanence; given the same conditions and you have the same relations. Thus the universal relation, the law, is seen to be the essential thing about an object. We no longer have a multitude of wholly separate things but a unity which comprehends differences within itself just as the law of the movements of the planets comprehends all the differences in the positions and rates of movement of the planets. Thus the rationality of nature is discovered, and our understanding ceases to be a mere capacity and is objectively realized. In the consciousness of law, that is, there is the consciousness of a unity which controls both the object and our consciousness of the object. Consciousness thus becomes self-consciousness.

78   The consciousness of law is the consciousness of a unity manifesting itself in and through differences, so that these differences are not separate things but the differentiations of a common principle. In the discovery of such a unity, consciousness finds itself and thus becomes self-conscious; or in becoming conscious of a universal, not simply an abstract universal or bare identity, but a concrete universal or ideality manifested in differences, the self is elevated to universality. At first consciousness seems separate from the object; there is simply a relation between the two. The object has one character and our ideas existing simply in consciousness may have any character. But in the discovery of this unity which underlies and controls differences, consciousness discovers that it is not arbitrary and accidental, that it cannot have any idea that it pleases; but that if it is to have real ideas, true ideas, it must regulate them according to unity, according to the necessary relations which constitute the object.

79   It is discovered, in other words, that consciousness has an objective content. But now this discovery of the necessary or the universal content of consciousness, this discovery of the unity of differences to which consciousness may conform, if it is really to be consciousness, makes self-consciousness. On the other side, it is discovered that objects are not a mere aggregate of particular things; that such objects are only appearances and that their reality lies in law, or in the unity of differences. Thus it is discovered, on the one hand, that consciousness is objective, that it can *be* consciousness only as controlled through certain objective and universal laws and relations, while on the other side, it is discovered that the consciousness involves a consciousness of the unity underlying them all, that is, self-consciousness. In the discovery, therefore, of the unity which controls and constitutes all different things, consciousness comes to itself; it becomes truly an I, or ego.

80   By the student of Kant this process of the elevation of consciousness to self-consciousness may be compared to Kant's deduction of the categories. In Kant there was the same attempt to show that the consciousness of self is dependent upon or mediated through consciousness of objects; that we cannot form an analytic judgment "I

am I," excepting through the synthetic judgment that the I has for its content a manifold of objects combined according to the necessary principles of union. On the other hand, Kant attempted to show that a consciousness of objects was possible only through synthetic necessary principles which combined the manifold of sense into a unity, and that the self was required in order to exercise this function of synthetic unity.

There is, however, a difference here between Kant and Hegel. Kant conceived of the self as a sort of uniting principle which somehow stood outside of the manifold and simply reduced it to connected form. He never was able, therefore, to reconcile self-consciousness with the consciousness of objects. Each was necessary to the other, yet[22] each always remained separate from the[23] other and even opposed to it. Self-consciousness was in itself formal and a mere point of unity having no content of its own. The objects could never be reduced to any final or unconditioned unity. But according to Hegel, the self is not a formal uniting activity, it is rather the organized unity of the objects themselves. It is not something required to give unity to an experience otherwise chaotic, but it is the real unity of the experience itself. The soul comes to self-consciousness when in its development, it realizes this unity which is forever involved in the constitution of the objective world. There is no real difference, then, between self and objective consciousness. Objective becomes self-consciousness the moment we realize the unity which controls it.

At first, however, we seem to have self-consciousness and the consciousness of objects; that is to say, we become conscious of the principle of unity long before we are able to carry out this unity into its details. We know that there is a unity and a universal in the object before we can tell what it is. Just so far as it occurs, the unity falls outside the multiplicity of objects and yet we know that this unity is only the unity of the objects themselves. There is, therefore, a contradiction; in principle the self and objects are one, as a matter of realized fact they are not. But they ought to be one. The self, in being conscious of the unity or universal, practically knows that all objects belong to itself, and yet so far as it has not concretely worked out their unity, so far they do not belong to itself.

83   Desire is the expression of this contradiction. Were man and the object wholly one, he would not desire it, and would always enjoy the full satisfaction, but on the other hand, were man and the object wholly separate he would never desire it. It would never occur to him that the object stood in any relation to him so that it could afford him any satisfaction, but because of the unity which exists in principle, although not realized in fact, man desires. The desire is thus the first step in the more concrete realization of the unity. In the satisfaction of the desire the independence of the object is negated; the object is made simply one element of the activity of the self, the object is translated into the subject. On the other hand, the self, in satisfying its desires, becomes active and thus ceases to be a mere capacity. Instead of being a mere I in general, it realizes itself by making the objects contribute to itself; thus the subjective becomes objective. There is a defect, however, in the satisfaction of desires through objects; desires are satisfied only through the destruction of the object. The very process of satisfying the desire annihilates the object which satisfies it, and thus there is the recurrence of another desire, and so indefinitely. Man can really satisfy himself only in an object which endures, in an object which is as permanent and universal as himself; hence the very attempt to realize himself, through annihilation of particular objects, that is to say, through the satisfaction of particular desires, involves a contradiction. But by the process of satisfying desires, man loses his mere subjectivity and becomes a definitely conscious self. He comes to recognition of self as an object, or he becomes conscious of an object which is not merely a thing but which is universal. Man therefore struggles to get recognition of himself. He finds himself one in the world of individuals each of whom is striving to obtain this recognition in order that he may realize his selfhood; in order, that is, that his self may not be simply something set over against objects, but that it may itself be truly objective.

84   In the first place, each individual attempts this other struggle by giving battle to every other self, each one attempts to reduce the other

to a thing or to a means for his own satisfaction. As a simple natural being, that is, as a particular self, consciousness limited to a particular time and place, self-consciousness contradicts itself. This merely natural being must therefore be destroyed, and through battle of each with others it is destroyed. Man, in becoming conscious that others are not things but persons, becomes conscious that he himself is a person. Only through this mutual struggle and resistance, then, is the consciousness of freedom evolved. At first, however, the struggle gives rise only to the condition of master and slave. This is not a recognition of the universality of the self or of the ego, but it is a necessary stadium in such recognition. The master learns that he must not destroy others but that he must care for them in order to be cared for himself. He recognizes, that is, that his free existence is dependent upon the existence of others and is not in hostility to other existences. The slave learns also to subordinate his own particular desires and ends to the wants of others; he learns to socialize to some extent his activity and thus becomes truly universal. But since we have here simply the dependence of one individual upon another individual, we have indeed a step beyond mere isolated individuality, but in the full recognition of the principle of selfhood. This can come about when the self exists not simply through other particular selves, but through the principle of selfhood involved in it all. The state of slavery or of serfdom expresses, that is to say, only a particular union of wills and a union which, therefore, is more or less external. The complete union of will or the true universality of self-consciousness can be brought about only when all are recognized as free. Slavish obedience forms thus the beginning of freedom, but since that which is obeyed is not the truly universal or rational self-consciousness in some other particular form, it is only a beginning of freedom.

 Full freedom is developed when the particular selves recognize that there is a true unity of will to which all equally owe obedience. This constitutes the transition to the universal self-consciousness which is the substance of every social organization. It is the spirit of the family, of the fatherland, of the state, the basis of all virtue, of love, friendship,

85

honor and fame. In this universal self-consciousness the particular self-consciousness learns that it can only be in and through its unity with others. It learns, in other words, that the true objective self is neither itself nor some other particular self, but is a unity which expresses itself in all these particular selves. Now then it is seen that self-consciousness is truly objective instead of being simply one object among or by the side of other objects. This unity of the self and objects, or the discovery that self is the true universal, and that there is no true objectivity excepting in and through unity of particular selves, constitutes reason. Reason, in other words, is a concrete unity of consciousness.

86   Hegel calls the third part of the doctrine of subjective spirit, that part which deals with reason, psychology. Reason is the spirit which divides itself, on the one side, into the universal self, and on the other into the object identical with it. This object is just as rational as reason is and reason is no longer an empty capacity but has a content which is itself objective. The process of reason is simply carrying out in detail the identity of itself with the object already known to exist in principle. This process has two sides; on one hand it is intelligence. Here the identifying movement comes from the object inwards toward the subject. It consists, in other words, in realizing a rationality of the object. When the unifying movement begins on the side of the subject and goes toward the object, we have will. Will is the objectifying of reason. The content, then, of both intelligence and will is the organic unity of subject and object. Intelligence gets this unity in the form of ideas or of meaning; in a form, therefore, which is somewhat one-sided. Will realizes the unity in an activity which is neither merely subjective nor merely objective, but in which both the idea and the existing object are included and transformed, thus constituting what we may term either a higher idea or a more adequate form of the object. Will, that is to say, is not merely an act of changing ideas into existences, but is the activity which comprehends within itself as factors both an idea and an object.

87   The activity of intelligence takes the form of knowledge. This is the process of translating that which seems to be given to thought

into a form of thought. Its end is to find reason, reason not in the abstract, but concrete reason, reason expressed in definite form. All so-called faculties of mind are simply stages in this development of knowledge. This process begins with feeling or sensation which we now come upon for a third time in a third way. In the first place, sensation was a condition of the soul, simply an experience with which the soul identified itself. In the second place, it was a form of consciousness; here the qualities of feeling were spread over the soul and projected into the form of an independent object. Now sensation is seen to be the primary realization of the unity of subject and object. Were subject and object really independent of each other no sensation would be possible. At the standpoint of the soul sensation seemed to be wholly subjective, at the standpoint of consciousness wholly objective, a property of the thing. We now see that it is both subjective and objective. In sensation the subject ceases to be mere subject or capacity and gets a certain objectivity, while the object on its side ceases to be brute thing or fact and gets a quality and a meaning for consciousness. Sensation, in other words, is a concrete reality which includes within itself both the abstract subject and the abstract object. So far as sensation is a stage in knowledge, reason is in and behind it just because sensation is an expression of the unity of subject and object.

Sensation is the stuff or material for all knowledge whatever. All our ideas and scientific notions of nature and of political and ethical relations, and all other religious ideas develop themselves out of their intelligence,[24] out of a condition of feeling. But this does not mean that intelligence was originally empty and that it has received all its content from without as something foreign to itself. On the contrary, all reason is latent or implicit in sensation and the development of the higher forms from sensation is simply the working out of the unity of the subject and object which is expressed in a rudimentary way in sensation, into more definite and adequate forms.

The activity of spirit in relation to this stuff of sensation first takes the form of attention. This distinguishes, breaks up the aims of sensation and gives its various elements an individuality of their own. In thus distinguishing sensations from each other spirit makes them external to each other or puts them in space and time. Space and time are thus, as Kant called them, forms of perception, but this does not mean that they are only subjective forms; they are true forms of the perceived objects themselves, for perception is just this activity of distinguishing objects and events from each other. The form of this distinction, if we separate it from what is distinguished, constitutes space and time, just as the what that is distinguished are objects in space and time. Neither of the two, then, can be separated from each other. Space and time are the general sides of the distinguishing, objects the particular side. But attention marks more than the breaking up of sensation into objects apparently external to itself; attention depends upon interest in the object and this interest means a certain unity of the object with self; we attend only to that which interests us, and only that interests us which is felt to be bound up within our own being.

90 Perception, as the outcome of attention to sensation, does not mean the recognition of a lot of particular objects distinct from the subject or self: that was what we had in the stage of consciousness. Perception, as we have it here, is intuition in the popular sense of that term, insight, getting hold of the real meaning of our experience. It is piercing through the outward shell of an object and seeing into its true value and meaning. It is not an act of some isolated faculty, getting hold of some isolated object, it is rather the whole man sensing the object, realizing its value. It is the state of mind illustrated in the attitude of the poet to some natural object, or of the practical man to some act. The practical man sees into the situation and therefore can tell what should be done. Perception in this sense has exactly the same object as thought. It is indeed simply a direct thought or judgment, a judgment which has not worked out its basis of reason.

91 But when intelligence has thus penetrated the inner meaning of an object, it has made it its own, it has internalized it, and thus we advance from the stage of presentation to representation, from perception to remembrance. In both the Latin and German languages, the words for memory have the sense of making an object inward or

a form of mind itself. The word "remember" has the same root as the word "mens" (Latin). We have the same idea conveyed in our word "mindful" and "remind"; here outer perception is changed into an inner idea. This is the stage between directly finding meaning or self in the object, that is, perception, and the reflective or reasoned finding of self, that is, thought.

There are various stages in the process by which the meaning of the object becomes part of the self. In the first place, we have involuntary memory. Here the content of the idea is exactly the same as the content of the perception. Union with mind is seen only in the fact that the mind can preserve its ideas; it is no longer directly dependent upon the actual presence of the object in space. But intelligence has, as it were, the object stored up within itself: the object, in other words, is changed into an image. The thing is transformed from an external space and time into a mental space and time. Through this process what is gained is a certain generality; the experience is relieved from its immediate limitations of space and time. By remembering an old experience the mind can have it in any space and at any time. But this gain in universality is accomplished with a loss of freshness and directness. So far as the image has the same content as the perception, so far the mind is not free in recalling it; the mind is not so thoroughly identified with this content that it can make it its own whenever it will. Remembering has to wait upon some other actual perception which restores the past experience. The universality of the image, in other words, is formal and external. So far as the self succeeds in identifying one of its experiences more completely with itself, so far the image is not dependent for its presence upon the actual presence of any object.

Intelligence gets the power of bringing from them this image, and thus involuntary memory becomes imagination which at first takes the form of reproductive imagination, which is exactly like memory in the images which it brings up, but unlike it in that the bringing up of these images is a matter of will. It is voluntary recollection. The mind does not have to wait for some actual perception to call up the image but it can manipulate its present experiences so as through them to call up a wished-for or past experience. By this the imagination forms trains of images, it relates the images to each other and by this process of relating images finally brings about generic ideas. That is, it associates this and that and the third experience of color so as to have a general idea of color. It brings the particular experience into a line or connection of experiences, and thereby gives it a certain degree of universality. This associating act of imagination constitutes the fantasy or symbolic imagination.

94 Here each image stands, not simply for itself as it does in memory and in reproductive imagination, but it stands also for the other images associated with it which may be developed from it. It comes to symbolize, that is to say, the whole train of ideas connected with it. Here, then, we have two sides: we have the image which is particular and so far sensuous, and we have also the movement of ideas back and forth from this idea, and this movement constitutes the generality of the image. The image is simply a sign or token. It no longer has value in itself but simply for what may be done with it for the train of ideas of which it is the starting point. The generic idea, then, is a sort of mixture of the particular and the universal. It is upon this stage that art arises, for art is precisely the embodiment of some universal value in a particular form which stands for, represents, or suggests that universal.

95 In fantasy, intelligence finds more complete expression; in perception and in the merely reproductive memory the inner side is related to intelligence but the existence seems to fall outside of intelligence. But in the image which symbolizes a universal idea, intelligence gives itself being: the form of the image as well as its content is the product of intelligence itself. Fantasy, in other words, is the mutual[25] in which the side of meaning or the universal and of existence, the side which is the mind's own, and that which is not found by the mind, the inner and the outer sides are completely shaped into one. In perception and reproductive memory, intelligence is a sort of indefinite chamber in which these forms exist, but in the true image intelligence is no longer that in which the ideas reside but it gets outward existence in particular form.

The fantasy expresses itself in various ways; first, there is the symbolizing fantasy. This is most dependent upon the actual perception, for it chooses for the expression of its general ideas some material whose own meaning is analogous to that of the general idea to be embodied. The allegory introduces more of the subjective element and treats the objective side somewhat arbitrarily. The poetic fantasy, while comparatively free from dependence on external material, can yet employ such sensual stuff as is adequate to the meaning of the idea to be embodied. But as imagination develops it comes from symbols to signs.

In the symbol the thing itself has a certain identity with the thing symbolized, but in the sign there is no such connection, the actual original meaning of the thing itself is done away with or is subordinated entirely into an expression of some idea. A flag or a gravestone, for example, means something entirely different from that which they immediately indicate. Symbols can be directly interpreted, signs have to be learned. There still is something sensuous left like the colors of the flag or the form of the gravestone, but this sensuous material has no value any longer for itself, but simply as standing for something else. The sign is the image which has received the independent idea of intelligence into itself for its very meaning.

Speech is the great achievement of the imagination at this stage. In speech, either written or spoken, the thing itself is degraded from its independent value and reduced to a means of showing forth or embodying some general idea of intelligence. Speech has thus necessarily two sides; on one side the sensuous stuff which is generalized by being made the means of expressing an idea. On the other hand, there is the general idea which loses its abstract generality by being incorporated into the particular sign which expresses it. Learning to read and write is, therefore, the sensual means of culture, since it lifts the spirit from the sensible concrete to pay attention to the universal or ideal element and thus, on the other side, enables the ideal element, which would otherwise remain latent or wholly internal, to express itself freely in outward form. Speech, therefore, as the embodiment of intelligence in a form which owes its meaning to intelligence, constitutes the transition to thought. This translation is realized in what Hegel calls memory proper.

99 This memory proper consists in gaining ability to control the particular name and sign, to get the meaning out of the sign into itself independently of the sign. Memory in the ordinary sense, or the mere ability to reproduce a past experience, consists in making external the meaning of some outward fact or perception. Memory proper, as Hegel uses the term, is the ability to make internal or get the meaning out of some sign. It bears the same relation to the sign, therefore, that the merely reproductive remembering bears to the thing. This memory proper Hegel takes up under three heads: first, memory which preserves the name, second, the reproductive, and third, the mechanical memory. The first means simply that when we see or hear a word we are capable of calling to mind the ideas which are objectively related to the thing; if we hear the word house, for example, it is not a mere sound which we take in but through the sound we appropriate to ourselves a certain set of objective relations or things.

100 2. Reproductive memory is that which has and knows in the name the thing itself without the use of any actual perception or any image of the thing. In the word "lion" we neither need an actual perception of any such animal nor any mental picture of the thing itself, but simply the name which, since we understand it, is the simple pictureless idea. If we had simply the imagination we would be able to produce only tableaus or panoramas of pictures, each one of which would stand to us for a certain idea. But in this reproductive memory we are freed from dependence upon the images and use simply the name itself which calls to us what we wish to know. Words are, then, the objective existence of our thoughts and this existence is absolutely necessary to our thoughts. We only know of our thoughts when we give to them an objective form, when we get them, as it were, outside our own inner being and get them out into spoken sounds or written words; thus they no longer belong simply to us as individuals, but get a certain universality of their own. The fact, then, that thought is so bound up with the word is not to be regarded as a lack in thought and as something unfortunate for thought; it is not true that the

inexpressible is the most valuable thing. The inexpressible thing is only something confused, it is an empty void which gets clearness and content only when it goes over into words. The dependence of thought, then, upon words is not an external accident. The dependence of thought upon words is simply thought's own necessity that it objectify itself and get concrete form. Just as true thought is a fact, so is the word when it is used by true thought. It is true that words lead astray and confuse, but this is not because they are words, but because of the erroneous and misleading thought back of them. So far as the mind becomes intelligent in its use of words so that it can deal with the words as things and deal with things through words, it ceases to be a subjective capacity and becomes itself a sort of thing.

3. In mechanical memory intelligence gets a certain outward existence and becomes itself a fact almost and is running by its own machinery. In mechanical memory the intelligence gets a certain outward expression working up its own processes and laws, it goes of itself as it were without dependence upon presentation. Ideas are consolidated into a fact. This transformation of mind into a thing forms the transition into a fact. Thought is the simple identity of the subjective and objective. It knows that that which is thought is, and that which *is* is only in so far as it is thought. Thought knows itself as the very nature of things; there is no longer a distinction between the thing and the meaning of the thing itself. Persons who do not understand philosophy throw up their hands at the absurdity of hearing it said that thought is being, yet the unity of thought and being lies at the basis of our activity.[26] As rational beings we must have this basis, but a distinction can be made as to whether we are thinking or whether we know ourselves as thinking. We are thinking beings under all circumstances, whatever, that is to say, thought is the content of all mental processes, but we know our thought only when it becomes pure thought, that is to say, when we get at the true meaning freed from all extrinsic circumstance. In ordinary thought, that which does not recognize itself as such, the elements of the thought are wrongly put together, they are disordered; but in pure or self-conscious thought we become conscious of the nature of our thinking and thus

not simply think, but regulate our thinking or think rightly. So far as we think rightly, we think on the basis of the act itself.

Thought is at first formal, it takes the material of perceptions and ideas and, abstracting a universal from them, re-imposes it then upon them; that is to say, formal thought begins with the process of abstraction which discovers the universal element present in particular cases and then goes on to generalization in which through the medium of this universal the particular facts are reduced to genera or classes; that is to say, thought appears here as formal since contrasted with the material thought about. It is the operation of thinking that is here meant by thought. This operation or form must be independent of the content. But after all this process of discovery, the universal is not arbitrary. If the universal is a true universal, it is not something separate from the particulars to be found by abstraction but is the meaning of the particulars themselves. Thinking is thus transformed from a process of abstraction into a process of deducing the true meaning of the facts themselves. The true meaning thus deduced is the universal. The universal is not something to be hitched on by further act to the particulars; it is the principle in the facts constituting their character. When this is discovered, thought ceases to be merely formal, a process of operation upon an outside material, and becomes one with the content of the facts themselves. Thought, when there is a difference between form and content, is termed understanding; when there is a unity, reason. The discovery of the complete objective character of thought constitutes the transition from theoretical to practical spirit. The process of working out or realizing the objective nature of our thought is will.[27]

Will, in other words, is thought conscious of its own unity and of its own activity in determining a content. This ability of thought to determine its own material constitutes the freedom of the will. So far as the will is the principle of unity, we have the formal will on the one side, and the particular inclination on the other. The distinction between the two forms is what we call freedom of choice; that is, thought can distinguish itself from any particular desire or, having distinguished itself, can proceed to identify itself with any particular inclination. This is our arbitrary or subjective freedom. Thought cannot be realized outwardly in any particular inclination but only through the universalizing of our inclination, through getting a satisfaction which meets, not one particular desire merely, but all. The struggle to reach this complete satisfaction is the struggle for happiness and is the transition from subjective to objective freedom. So far, in other words, as spirit actually realizes itself through particular inclinations, so far it becomes something objective. This constitutes the transition from subjective to objective spirit. Free spirit is actual spirit, that is to say, spirit in which the unity of thought has expressed itself not simply in principle as an abstract unity, but has organized itself in and through particular inclinations and desires.

The idea of freedom of the individual, as such, came into the world with Christianity. Previous to that time men had known only that man was free by birth or by culture or by philosophy and learning or something of that sort, but according to Christianity the individual as such has an infinite value, since he is the object and end of the love of God; since, that is to say, he is the object in which all the forces of nature and of history culminate, since he is their active out-working. When religion teaches that man, as such, has a relation to absolute spirit and that this relation constitutes the very essence of man, religion also teaches that the divine spirit is actually present in the sphere of the world's existence, that it is the very substance of the State and Family. The relation of the individual will to the absolute unity, therefore, changes its character. In the sphere of the subjective, spirit seemed after all to fall outside of the individual; it was something which the individual was after, something which he was striving to get or which he ought to get. But so far as it is discovered that the absolute will is expressed in the world and in social institutions, so far the mere striving for something beyond ceases. The objective will or freedom is already there, and the individual instead of striving for something beyond, has only to appropriate the wealth of spirit already present in the institutions about him.

The discussion of objective will falls under three heads: First, that of spirit and law; secondly, the nature of morality; and thirdly, the nature of the ethical world as the unification of outward law and of rights and of the inner intentions and motives. The idea which underlies the whole discussion is that the rational will is one with the particular will and the whole process of the objective spirit is simply the process of working out this identity involved from the very start. Man is free from the start, but none the less he has to work out or realize his freedom. This realization, however, is no reaching for something beyond which man merely ought to be, it is the continued free movement of taking home to himself that which he already is in principle.

106   In the sphere of rights and law we have the fact of the existence of free will; that will is no longer subjective but is an objective fact possessing, therefore, universality, is testified to by the existence of laws and rights. Law and right constitute, in other words, the objective system of man's freedom. In the sphere of rights the individual will is a person; personality is a particular will which at the same time knows itself to be universal. This personal will first finds expression of its universality through *property*. The merely subjective will has nothing, it is simply an inner capacity of action, but let the will realize itself in some objective content and then it has or knows something. Property, in other words, is the first stage in the realized will or objective freedom. So far as man owns things, so far they cease to be limitations upon his will and become tools or instruments through which his will expresses itself. Property is the penetration of nature by personality. This explains two main facts regarding property:—First, that an individual permanently appropriates something to himself, and, secondly, that others recognize this appropriation. Animals use things and they even store them up for future use, but they do not in any true sense have property, they do not express themselves in the realm of nature. They have, that is to say, no universal or permanent element in their will, and thus are not able to give themselves permanent objectifications. It is because of the presence of this same universal element in property that others recognize the appropriation once made. Property then involves not only the expression of one individual will, but many. Nothing is really owned unless the equalization is recognized by others. The thing owned is thus a middle ground upon which different

wills meet. Were the act of equalization simply the act of a particular will there would be no property at all. The very fact that others recognize the equalization shows that they help constitute it. In an ultimate sense it is just as much their appropriation as that of the individual who formally acquires it.

The mutual relation instituted between different wills by property finds higher expression in the act of contract. Contract is simply the explicit recognition of what is already involved in property. It is the express agreement of two wills to recognize each other through the intermediary of some thing just as property is the implicit recognition. But while property, and thus contract, are means of uniting various individual wills, means of transforming them into a unity of wills, they are at the same time means of bringing about conflict. In property and in contract the individual wills are only external in reality to each other, they are not one in themselves, one in their inner being and purpose, but only as realities to some outward thing. Under two circumstances there would never be any conflict between different wills: there would be no conflict if they all had the same interest and purpose; but neither would there be any conflict if, having different purposes, these purposes never found outward expression. In its own inner nature each will would be entirely inaccessible to every other, but in the outward thing, appropriated by will, the spheres of the individual wills come into contact and thus into conflict with each other. Different persons may under different circumstances all acquire a right to the same thing and thus there comes about a conflict of rights. This violation of right may be unintentional, that is, the individual may assert his claim in good faith, or the individual may consciously assert his individual will as against the known rights of others, thus constituting actual wrong, the bad will. Here the will has violated its own law, that of universality. This universal character of will, however, is still there and must assert itself. This it does in punishment; punishment, that is to say, is the reassertion of the will in its own true principle against any particular act violating its principle. In appearance the punishment may be inflicted by others; in truth it is inflicted by a man upon himself. The deed, since the violation of the very law of will comes to nothing, and this abstraction of the act, its reduction to nothingness, is punishment.

108 The philosophy of punishment, then, is that it is the negation of some particular act of will by means of its reference to a universal principle of law. This universal principle not lying outside the act is the revelation of the act itself. So far we have been dealing with the expression of the will in external form; through this process of punishment we are led to see that the will has its own inner principle, its universal, which cannot be violated without some compensating external act by which the principle again asserts itself. This discovery of the will of its own inner principle as universal leads us from the sphere of abstract law to a second division of objective spirit, namely morality.

109 Another way to make the transition from abstract law to morality is as follows: The movement of will is towards the realization of the universality of will in particular persons by bringing them to common interests and purposes and thus to real unity of action. In the sphere of abstract rights and laws, this unity is sought to be obtained in the region mainly of external acts or rather of acts on their external side. But external acts are particular, and thus as external they cannot be completely adjusted to one another. Taken simply as so many acts, one must inevitably encroach upon the territory of another, thus giving rise to conflict. Punishment is the solution of this conflict and thus the restoration of the unity, but punishment itself is another external particular act and thus itself leads to conflict. The only way of escaping, then, this conflict of various acts, the only way of uniting them into a real whole, is by discovering a principle. They are unified, not as so many particular acts, but on the basis of some single principle or inner motive from which all proceed. This, then, is the sphere of morality, discovery and the working out of the inner law of the will's action. While the sphere of objective rights is the sphere of the relation of persons to each other in their outward acts, the sphere of morality is the sphere of man's relation to himself; the inner sphere of his inner motives and purposes and the necessity of the transition

from abstract rights to morality is that a man cannot really settle his relation to others in particular cases until he has, once for all, settled his relation to himself.

Historically, we may mark the transition from rights to morality in the epoch of the Sophists and of Socrates in Greece. The older Greek morality had been entirely a morality of custom. It was regulated by social expectation and by instituted social forms. These prescribed for a man what he should do and at the same time assured him freedom in the performance of his duties. The morality was that of external acts rather than that of inner principles. The Sophists became conscious of this fact on its negative side; Socrates became conscious of it on its positive. The Sophists, that is, seeing that this current morality was simply a matter of custom, declared that all morality was simply a matter of convenience and agreement, its only sanction being the power of some one who insists that this convention must be kept. Aside from the force which backs the convention the latter has no binding force at all. Socrates practically agreed with the Sophists in denying the value of a merely outward morality, of that based on the conventional life or the customary acquiescence to prescribed duties. But he added a new and positive principle, viz.: that morality proceeded from man's own intelligence; that for an act to be moral it must proceed from a man's intelligent recognition of some end; that an unexamined life is not to be led by man. This was Socrates' great contribution to ethics. He transferred morality from the realm of outer acts fixed by custom and institutions to the inner motive fixed by the individual's own intelligent judgment. The ground and source of all virtue, according to him, was in wisdom or knowledge. This was simply the historic recognition by man that the will does not find adequate expression in a series of external acts but that there must be some principle of intelligence which controls and unifies these acts. The search for this principle, the search for the law of will, thus becomes the problem of morality, both of practical conduct and in systematic, ethical treatises.

The moral will, as distinct from the abstract and jural will, has its own rights. This right is primarily that every act be of a man's own proposal or design. The principle of the jural will was that there were certain other persons to whose acts one's own conduct must be adjusted. The principle of morality is that every person is himself a will, that this will of his own has an infinite value and that, having this infinite value of its own, it must look at matters for itself and decide its own ends for itself. My every act must, in other words, be my act, it must proceed from my recognition of what I consider to be good for myself. So far as the act does not depend upon my own examination of the circumstances and from my own choice, so far the act is not mine at all. Indeed it is not an act, truly, but simply an event which occurs. Every act, in other words, in order to be an act must be based on some aim, purpose or design which is the agent's own. Hence the conjunction of responsibility with action.

Now, at first this design may have very little content; it may be arbitrary, capricious or highly individualistic. The motive may be simply a chance idea which comes into the head of the agent and is then acted upon. The action once performed, however, has outward consequences going far beyond the original immediate aim; thus a child may mean only to play with matches, and yet the outward consequences of his act may be the burning down of his father's house. So far as the outward consequences of an act are noticed, they re-act upon the original aim, extending it and enlarging it, they make it more general. So far as an act is seen to have certain consequences necessary to be with it, so far the design of that act is universalized, the consequences which would result from the act become its law. The aim is thus transformed into an intention. The agent can no longer think simply of a particular act which he was going to perform but must take into account all the consequences which he sees likely to result from it, this conception of consequences being itself further enlarged to the idea of happiness or of welfare as the end of conduct. Each act has its own particular consequence, indeed, but more than this every act has its side in which it re-acts upon the interests of the agent. All acts, whatever, then, can be viewed from their relation to the agent's happiness. This happiness may be regarded as the final controlling intention of the will. So far as any act does not meet some interest of the agent, so far it is wholly valueless. This is the right of the particular subject to find himself satisfied, to get his own satisfaction and to get it in his own way, not having to take either his ideals or his means from another person, it is the right of subjective freedom.

This idea is the turning point from the ancient to the modern world; this right was first brought out in its whole meaning in Christianity. The ideas of love, the romantic ideas, eternal happiness or salvation as the aim of the individual and conscience, all belong to this development. This welfare does not belong, however, to any particular will. All wills, since the expression of the same principle, have the same right to their own satisfaction, and thus the well-being, the happiness of other individuals, is also a social end to the agent. So far as the individual learns that he must control his conduct not simply by the idea of his own happiness but also by the happiness of others, so far he gets the idea of the good; the conception of good, in other words, is the conception of the universal law of will realized in a particular will.

This good stands in a double relation to the particular will; on the one hand every individual has a right to know his own good. That which he is to recognize as valid must be seen by the agent himself to be good, and an act is to be reckoned by an agent as right or wrong, good or bad, just according to his own knowledge of the value of the act. The good exists absolutely only in thought and through thought. Nothing is merely good to a man but thinking makes it so, and this right to recognize nothing which I do not myself see into as rational is the highest right of the subject. So far, however, since the person's insight may be true or false, the principle is somewhat subjective and formal.

On the other side, therefore, there is the right which the object has to be recognized in its own rationality, that is to say, while the agent has the right to recognize the act for himself, he has a duty to use all means at his command to form the best possible judgment of what is right. This control of his judgment by the rationality of the subject matter is what Hegel calls the right of the object. The good, in other words, constitutes the very essence of the individual's own will and because it constitutes the essence of his own will, it obligates him, it is his duty. So far as the good takes the form of simply the abstract universal or principle of will, so far it is duty at large. To do one's duty for duty's sake means to do some act on account of the universal principle of will without recognizing clearly this universal principle of reality in the particular act, but the good cannot remain thus general abstraction; so far as it does do so it gives rise to the idea of the mere ought or of the opposition between the ought and the is. This puts the particular over against the universal because it has not fully worked out the concrete meaning of the universal. So far, in other words, as a man has not brought home to himself in particular specific ways what his true good is, so far this good seems to be somewhat beyond his particular actions imposing a law upon them. So far as he can translate his good into particular acts, so far it becomes his interest as well as his duty to perform the specific act. The good ceases to be an abstract law of obligation and becomes the actual controlling motive of the act itself. In other words, the stage of doing a duty for the sake of a duty marks the point in the morality at which a man is sufficiently moralized to see that there is a good which should control his actions, but not sufficiently moralized to bring this good home to himself as his own good in every specific act.

116. The process of translating the abstract idea of good or of duty into concrete terms, of bringing it into relation, that is, with the special acts, is the conscience. In other words, conscience is thought brought to bear upon matters of conduct. Conscience expresses the absolute right of subjective will to know, in itself and from itself, what is right and what is duty; but whether the conscience of a given individual is correct, whether, that is to say, what he holds for right is actually right depends, not upon the form of his judgment, but upon its content. Right and duty are themselves the rational or individual elements of the will and they cannot, therefore, be either the particular property of an individual nor be brought home to him in the form of mere feelings, the so-called moral sense. Conscience, in other words, has a law. It must be true and conscience is not conscience

strictly as long as it remains simply an opinion any more than in a physical science a man's opinion of truth is a sufficient guaranty of truth; conscience, in other words, as a principle of action, is still somewhat subjective and formal. We have not mastered the true meaning of conscience until we have seen how the power of knowing and deciding what is good becomes a real power, by what means it actually gets hold of the truth. In itself, conscience, so far as the moral law stands outside of it as something which ought to be, may go this way or that. The particular will, that is to say, may adapt itself somewhat to its own private inclinations and desires for its end, or it may take the universal for its end. In this relation, then, of the individual will to the universal law, in the relation of the conscience to the ought, evil arises as well as good. The particular and the universal are apart, and so far as they are apart their unity is simply something which ought to be but which need not be as a matter of fact. Only when the individual will and the universal law are really together does the will find full realization, and the good become an actual fact instead of something which ought to be. The sphere in which the individual will and the universal law are identified, and identified not in any abstract way but in individual concrete actions and interests, constitutes the realm of the ethical world as distinct from that either of abstract rights or abstract morality.

In abstract rights the emphasis is upon the claim which the individual will has, claims upon nature, claims upon other wills. The point is that the will, since the expression of the personality, has a certain independent sphere of action within which it is supreme, so that if any other will encroaches, it has a right to punishment. In the sphere of morality the emphasis falls upon the other side, it is the idea of duty, not that of rights (which is emphasized). The claim is no longer of one person upon others, but rather it is the claim of the law as universal will upon all persons. The surrendering of private interests to the universal law is demanded. The universal appears as something beyond the particular person to which he should conform his conduct. In the ethical world the two ideas of right and duty are one. The individual interest no longer has to be sacrificed to the general law as an accidental or even unworthy element. The particular self-interest is identified with the law, and the law is no longer an abstraction which ought to be, but lives in individuals as the very essence and substance of their own life and interests. In other words, the individual finds his full motive neither in some abstract right of his own nor in some abstract moral law. The will finds true expression neither in the sphere of independent activity of the will nor in an abstract universal law which controls all wills. The will finds complete expression only when it gets realized in actual institutions and when these institutions are so bound up with the very life purposes of the individual that they supply him his concrete motives.

118   The law is no longer abstract and it is no longer something beyond the individual nor is it any longer something which ought to be. In the first place it is the life and movement of existing social institutions, and in the second place it is concrete. These institutions, since they are actual existences, furnish the definite and specific conditions under which action must take place. What would be, say, the abstract law of justice, is through these institutions differentiated into the special circumstances which require one to act justly. And in the third place, since the individual is a member of these institutions, and can live his own life only in and through these institutions, they are one with himself, they are his true good. It is in performing his own function, taking his own position with reference to these institutions that he truly becomes himself and gets the full activity of which he is capable. It is this union, then, of the subjective and objective sides, of the particular will and the universal, of self-interest and law, which constitutes the essential character of the ethical world.

119   The will finds this ethical realization in three stages: the family, civil society and the State. The family is the ethical spirit of humanity in its most direct and sensuous form. Its principle is love, which means a will in which the opposition of self and others has passed away so that each member of the family satisfies himself only so far as he gives satisfaction to the other members of the family. The family is the direct or natural form of the ethical spirit because this unity is felt rather than comprehended. The basis of the family is the natural

wants and appetites of man, and these wants transformed through being made the instruments of a common good and a common life. As sensation is the first expression of knowledge, so love is the first expression of the ethical consciousness. All later knowledge is latent in sensation, but in sensation its real meaning is not brought out, so in love all higher forms of ethical union are latent but are not developed. The family, in other words, emphasizes too much the side of unity, not allowing full play to the principle of difference, and thus not after all realizing the highest principle of active unity which can come only when all individualities are allowed to develop themselves to the utmost.

The transition from the family to civil society comes about in just this way. As children grow up they recognize their own independent individuality and thus cease to be held together by the natural bond of the family. If the family endures, it is a voluntary re-adjustment of independent wills and not as one substance held together by a pervading spirit. Civil society thus emphasizes the state of difference of particular individuals just as the family emphasizes the side of the common factor.[28] Civil society is the realm of particular self-interest. The arena for the combat of the private interest of all against all. Will appears here in the form of external government restricting the play of this individual interest. To the private individual it seems simply a constraining force or else a means towards his personal advantage and security: the latter, so far as it affords free play to his self-interest, and the former so far as it keeps him from infringing on the self-interest of someone else. But this external government exercises an educating influence upon the individual and at the same time brings him to see that his true interest is public rather than private, it makes him see that his interest is not hostile to, but one with, that of others.

The region of civil society is also the realm of the system of wants or of industrial society. In society wants arise which are not simply individual or animal, but which are social, they are wants, that is to say, which are conditioned by the fact that the man wanting is a member of some social organism. In order to satisfy these wants we have labor which is also essentially social. In order to follow and meet men's wants, this labor has to be specialized, and thus there comes about the division of labor, through which the satisfaction of each is made dependent upon the labor of others; thus individuals are knit together through their mutual dependencies. So far as this comes about so that the given product does not satisfy simply the agent who produced it but makes for the satisfaction of others, and through others, for the satisfaction of society as a whole, we have wealth, which is the social fund. It is the very essence of civil society that the individual will, animally and outwardly having only his private interests which he aims to satisfy, yet only can satisfy these private interests by contributing to the satisfaction of others by producing wealth as distinct from mere property.

Through the inequality of individuals in relation to this social fund arise the classes of society. These are three: the Agricultural, where the social wants and activities stand in most direct dependence upon natural forces, where, that is to say, there is little play of thought; secondly, the Industrial class, the artisan and trading class, where reflection enters in more largely, taking the results of the agricultural class and by invention and machinery transforming them both in nature and in place for the satisfaction of social wants; and, thirdly, the class having charge of the general interests of civil society, the educators, priests and civil authorities. The latter class, being most remote from immediate dependence upon nature, have freedom to devote themselves more specially to the higher spiritual interests and to the control of society. The main difference between ancient and modern society is that in ancient society these classes were fixed simply on the basis of their objective rationality. That is to say, this division of classes is not accidental but determined by the very development of will itself; but the place of any given individual in one of these classes was not determined in ancient times by any rational principle, it depended upon some external accident, like birth. In modern times, while the differentiation of classes is still recognized, the given individual finds his place in one of these classes not by external law, but according to his own subjective capacities and inclinations. It is the principle of this union of outward law and subjective choice which gives the modern State its great stability as compared with the ancient.

In the arrangement of classes and the various individuals in the classes, we have the civil order which is conditioned upon justice and its demonstration. Thus there comes into being the State on its external side as government which correlates law as the requirement of the whole with the private interests of the individual. But this government is only the external side of a true organic unity. This constitutes the State where the individual identifies himself with the will manifested in the community in which he lives and thus gets beyond his mere individuality and becomes a member and organ of the whole. The State is then the completed objective spirit, the externalized reason of man; it reconciles the principle of law and liberty, not by bringing some truce or external harmony between them, but by making the law of the whole the prevailing interest and controlling motive of the individual. The state may be considered in three phases:—First, on its internal side with its special organization and constitution, secondly, in its true relations or dealings with other states, and thirdly, with relation to the generic principle of the organic active humanity as expressed in any particular state.

This latter point of view leads us on to the philosophy of history. In the internal constitution of the state Hegel considers chiefly the so-called functions or powers of the state. According to him these have a rational necessity. The legislative power is the side of universal will; the executive that which applies the universal will to particular cases and persons; and then, thirdly, the princely power which corresponds to the individual. Here the universal and particular elements are brought together into a single unity. This portion of Hegel's philosophy of the state has often been termed simply a philosophical extraction and justification of the then existing Prussian monarchy. While this, perhaps, is saying too much there can be no doubt that Hegel's discussion of the internal organization of the state is the most artificial and the least satisfactory portion of his political philosophy. He makes the ideal State most highly realized in the constitutional monarchy in whose structure simple monarchy, aristocracy and democracy are simply subordinate phases.

125 The guarantee of the constitution, that is, the organization of the state, lies in the spirit of the people themselves. Laws are rational and are executed just so far as the people come to self-consciousness. The constitution and its development is nothing but the process by which the nation becomes aware of the inner rationality of its own existence. The question then why and how an organized authority gets the right to make a constitution is like asking what makes the spirit of a people. It is perfectly absurd to separate the constitution from the national spirit, as if the national spirit could exist or ever have existed without possessing the constitution which is adapted to it. A constitution has never been made; it has developed itself out of the national spirit along with the development of that spirit itself.

126 The living totality which maintains and continually develops the state and its constitution is the government, the sovereignty in the truest sense of the term. The government is the universal side of the constitution; it is that side of the national organization which has the maintenance of the parts of the state for its intentional end, and at the same time it comprehends and realizes the universal ends of the whole which stand above the particular purposes of the parts, such as the family or civil societies.

127 On one side, then, the state is the national spirit of some particular people having their definite spot on the earth and their definite period in history. As a particular state it is exclusive in its relation to other states. In other words, the whole spirit of humanity is not embodied in any particular state. Hence the necessity of international relations which are simply a growth of one state of organized humanity. Because also each particular state is limited in space and time, it has a history; it is simply one epoch or stage in the larger world spirit. The state in its independence and separation is not true to its real meaning and therefore it passes away. Thus Hegel goes on from the philosophy of State to the philosophy of History as the highest manifestation of the objective spirit. The movement of history is the continuous freeing of spirit. It is the process by which the end and aim

of the world becomes conscious of itself, and in becoming conscious of itself secures the conditions of its own expression and thus becomes truly free. Since this development goes on in time the national states are the particular factors and stages of it. Each state brings forth some one factor in the continuous movement toward freedom.

It is presupposed, then, in the very treatment of history, that the world has an end or aim. History can be written or understood only as the development of this end. This is sometimes objected to as making history purely *a priori*, the arbitrary stating[29] of events according to some principle which the historian happens to record as the end to be realized in history. It is insisted that on the contrary the historian must be impartial, that he must pay no heed to any end, but simply record the facts themselves as they come. But this is absurd. Every history must have its own object or else it has no point; it would not even be so much as a child's fairy tale, for children require a certain point in their stories; there must be a certain unity to which the various events are related. The demand is correct, however, so far as it implies that this end of history is not to be supplied by the arbitrary reflection of the historian. The historian is to find the reason in history itself, and this reason in its own law or development constitutes the end or object with reference to which all historical events are to be ordered. The complete finding out of the reason or law immanent in history itself, whose development accounts for and explains the various peoples and epochs of history, constitutes the philosophy of history. This end is nothing less than the development of the spirit itself, the realization of its full capacities. So far as this occurs we have freedom, and therefore the end of history may be said to be freedom. The story of history is telling the tale of the development of man's freedom, the coming to consciousness by man, and the action which results from this mastering consciousness of himself. Man becomes free as he learns to know himself, for as he knows himself he masters himself, and in mastering himself he masters nature, making it one element in his own activity.

Progress in the consciousness of freedom is progress, then, in the consciousness of the absolute reason or spirit which is unfolding throughout all history; it is what religion calls God. History is the record of the continuous creation of God in consciousness just as physical science is the record of his continuous creation in the conscious realm. Any particular people can be understood only when viewed from the standpoint of the freedom or complete self-consciousness, and of the part which this particular nation plays in realizing true freedom. The fault of history is that in and through the passions and inclinations of particular men, in their apparent subjective choices, there is still working a larger law to which these particular desires and acts contribute. While a man may be thinking of his own particular ends and purposes, still the content of his act must be something larger, something which reaches far beyond the limits of his own individuality, and which contributes to the freedom of the whole. On the other hand, just so far as the individual becomes conscious of this larger content, so far as he becomes conscious of the end of the whole and identifies himself with it, so far he actively participates in the whole. In other words, every man and every nation has two sides. On one side, they are simply means or tools. So far as they are conscious of the full meaning of their motives and deeds, so far the larger end is simply working through them and utilizing them for itself. But so far as they become conscious of this larger law and are identified with their own action, so far they are themselves the end.

130   Before going on to the philosophy of the particular states, Hegel considers not only the development of the spirit but its relation to nature as conditioned upon geographic and climatic considerations. The spirit of a nation is always in close connection with its natural surroundings. The human spirit takes up into itself the surrounding necessities. Nature may either stunt or further the development of the spirit. So far as nature supplies man's wants easily, so far it affords him the leisure to think about himself, relieving him from the pressure of external conditions. In three separate instances the dependence of the development of the spirit upon geographical considerations may be seen. First, the dry up-lands which are the home of patriarchal life, nomadic existence, and without any fixed

political relations. It is second, in the valley plains, where nature is more fruitful, and we have the shepherd life replaced by agricultural, and great states founded. Thirdly, it is in the coast region, where human intercourse is facilitated instead of hindered, where the cycle of political development is completed.

There was no history simply because man existed: history began only when man came to know himself, when he became a conscious object of interest and of action to himself. Thus history in the subjective and the objective sense coincide. Peoples who have left no historical records of their existence, even in books, monuments, or some outward sign, cannot have had any true history. The very fact that they left no record shows that they were not conscious of themselves and therefore could not have had any history. The Oriental is the sign of history's childhood; it is here that spirit first becomes conscious of itself. It becomes aware of itself, however, only in a general and vague way. It only knew that there was spirit, law and power in general without realizing what this meant in individuals. Thus the Oriental world only knew that one was free. As in religion, so in politics, it was despotic. The Grecian world is the second period in history. Here it is recognized that some are free. It is not seen that the universal spirit is individualized in every man, but it is seen that it must be expressed in individuals and not simply in some one vast, dread power. Thirdly, in the Germanic nations and through the introduction of Christianity there arises the consciousness that the only definite spirit is embodied in every man and hence that all are free.

131

Omitting what is said about the Oriental world, we may illustrate Hegel's general treatment, first, by some points taken from the Grecian world. Greek life is the youth of spirit; it gives us the joyous view of the youthful freshness of spiritual life. In Greece the spirit was not simply lost in nature, as it is in the Oriental world, nor yet has it set itself free from nature, rising above it. On the contrary, it is directly at one with nature. There is a balance, an equilibrium, between nature and spirit. The spirit finds itself everywhere embodied and reflected in nature, hence the joyous and artistic character of Greek life. The typical sign of the Greek world is what Hegel calls the existence

132

of beautiful spiritual individualities, meaning by this that the individuals are neither sunk in a single over-shadowing power nor yet are conscious of themselves as individuals with ends of their own. As against the first view they are conscious of themselves, as against the second, they are conscious of themselves only as one with the laws and religious ideas of their time.

133 The creations of the Greek spirit flow from the spiritual individuality of Greek character. They are all works of art. These creations of art may be summed up under three heads,—First, man regards himself, his own body, as a work of art; and hence the culture which the Greeks bestowed upon their body in order that the natural body might be one with the indwelling spirit. Second, the objective work of art which took the form of the creation of other gods, the poetic mythology of the Greeks. The Greek gods were neither one absolute free spirit nor yet vast overpowering natural forces. They were themselves free individualities; they were the Greek individuals themselves idealized into greater beauty of life. They are neither natural forces nor mere symbols of such forces, they are complete individuals. The unity of the whole was conceived by the Greek only in the form of Fate, and outside blind necessity ruling all, even the lives of the gods.

134 The highest artistic creation of Greek spirit was, thirdly, their political creation, the state. To the Greek the state was his own nature. The spirit of the whole was the conscience of the individual. He had no private conscience. The laws of the state were not the declarations of some private will nor yet the outcome of reflective discussion. They were the natural outgrowth and flowering of the state itself.

135 Because the Greek had not become conscious of the universality of spirit but simply of his own individuality, he could not realize either that the whole of life was spiritual or that all classes of men were free. He therefore separated the economical side of life from the ethical. He held that man had two classes of wants: the natural, as for food, shelter, etc., labor for whose satisfaction was not ethical, and therefore degrading; and truly spiritual wants which related to art, the state, and free intercourse. In order that these spiritual wants might be supplied, there must be provided a basis in a substratum of

material good. Those who supplied this basis were outside the ethical life and hence were rightly treated as slaves. Only men with spiritual wants and ethical satisfactions were truly free.

The decline of Greek life came through the growing recognition of the universality of spirit and through the development of the subjective freedom which this necessitated. The Greek individual had his life only in and with the substance of the state. But with the growth of reflective self-consciousness he came to consider himself apart from the state and thus severed himself from the very substance of his being. He had so long been one with the life of the state that when distinguished from it he could no longer thrive. The Greek spirit had to pass away because it had never come to the consciousness of that principle of individuality which was its very basis. Just because its morality was directly[30] through the union of the individual with the state, just because spirit and nature were directly one, just because all its products were artistic, just because of all these things the Greek spirit was at once healthy, fresh and choice and at the same time limited. The removal of this limitation through the growth of reflective self-consciousness marked the decay of Greek life.

136

In Greek life the universal and the particular, the spiritual and the natural, have been at one; and thus characteristic forms of Greek life find expression as works of art. In Rome this naturalness and wholeness of life is at an end, the spiritual and the universal have gained the preponderance over the material, they have become separated from the particular. As Greece is the artistic spirit of the world, so Rome is the practical. Rome finds definite particular, elementary problems on hand and endeavors to solve these by rules. Greece was the poetry, Rome the prose of life. These rules take the form of rigid, abstract and general ideas. The genius of Rome is essentially demonstrative, it organizes empires, military and legal, through a detailed system of rules and regulations. The Roman empire in which civilized mankind is brought under one uniform law to which are subject not only the most diverse individuals but also the most diverse nations is simply one expression of the growing consciousness of the universal in Roman history. In Greece there

137

had been no law over the individual, the individual and the law were at one in the spirit of the family and the state. Roman mythology shows the same trait. Their gods, instead of being free individualities, are rather personifications of mental abstractions. But while this tendency toward the abstract universal gives a certain limitation and harshness to Roman life, it also gives to Rome its practical efficiency. These fixed, uniform rules were the weapons with which Rome conquered the world, mastering it in detail.

The outcome of the Roman principle is seen in the development of the empire. Here we have on one side a universal rule including within itself all varieties and aspects of life. On the other side are the individuals having politically, or with respect to this universal over them, no status, but yet having as individuals in their relations to one another a standing which the Greek, much less the Oriental, never attained. In Rome, men were recognized as legal individuals, as persons. Each individual was conscious of having certain rights in himself as an individual, as on an equality with other individuals and having power to enforce his rights as against them. While there has been less in the consciousness or oneness with the social organism, while indeed the living unity of this social organism has been abstracted into a uniform absolute law over the individual, yet there has been gain in the individual's consciousness of himself as a person.

This very divorce between the state and the individual at the same time emphasized both in becoming separated from each other; each gained in distinctness, but this separation meant a gulf in man's consciousness of himself. The more the individual became conscious of himself as an individual, having his own center of thought and will, having his own rights and duties, the more he became conscious of the emptiness of his individuality, since the living unity of the state in which alone he could find satisfaction was outside him. This contradiction between the individual infinity on the one side, that is, as respects other individuals, and yet as[31] absolutely limited on the other because without the sense of his organic unity with them, constitutes the misery of the later Roman world. The problem is how the empty form of individuality may be filled and satisfied, how, without renouncing the conception of the individual as a self-centered unit of action, the idea of the social relations may be brought home to him so that his connections with mankind can become the content of his activity.

The misery resulting from the contradiction in the conception of the individual and the resulting problem which this pain forces upon man were the preparation for Christianity. The conception of Christianity was that of the individual, this self-centered personality, not in his isolation or exclusion, but as a manifestation of the absolute unity of nature and of history, that is, as an incarnation of the divine spirit. It was in[32] this consciousness that personality consisted, not in isolation from others, but in union with them, that lay the essential principle of Christianity and which was the secret of its redeeming force. Mankind, without reasoning it out and seeing in any detailed way the consequences involved in the conception of the unity of God and man, yet felt a new faith and joy in its confidence of its attained unity with the source of all power and life. This Christian conception, then, comprehends within itself both the Greek and Roman principles and offers the means of reconciling the two. It gives us again the complete unity of Greek life where the individual feels himself at one with the state instead of at odds with it but it gives also the principle of Roman life in which the individual feels his own universality or absolute worth. The Christian principle involves the unity of man with the state because it shows that man is himself an embodiment of the absolute spirit, but it also involves the infinite value of the individual to himself for the very reason that he is this embodiment of absolute spirit.

Modern history consists, then, in the working out of this Christian principle in its definite, outward realization. We may recognize at least three periods in this realization. First, when the principle was expressed on the subjective side, was grasped by the intellect in the form of theology. Second, in the attempt to realize it in a specific outward form or in the church as an institution. Third, the realization of the contradiction involved in the attempt to express the Christian principle in some one specific institution and hence the virtue to express the principle in a universal way. This latter principle had naturally a negative and a positive side. Its negative side was the attempt to overthrow all special forms of belief and all special institutions so far as they limited the universal principle. The positive side was the organic reconstruction of intellectual and social life in accordance with the Christian idea.

142 The theoretical development of the Christian principle in the form of dogma occurred before its use as an organizing power in the region of political life. This was of course inevitable. The Christian principle was still confronted by the immense mass of existing social institutions which apparently rested upon another basis. Before the Christian principle could make effective headway against this objective structure it had to abstract itself and become conscious of its own meaning. Thus the early development is almost entirely subjective. It consisted in comprehending the new idea as an idea, a formulated statement.

143 As, however, the old political and social institutions passed away, or at least passed away so far as their external form was concerned, as they did at the fall of Rome, the Christian principle found a chance for finding outward expression and dominion. This chance was furthered by the fact that the peoples with whom it had to deal were the new barbarian Germanic peoples, the people who combined a wonderful mass of subjective feeling and capacity with an entire absence of all settled social organization or rational form in their life. In the contact of the Christian principle with the Germanic nations there met on one side the subjective factor of feeling which was aware of large possibilities eager for action; and on the other side a body of objective, recognized and stable truth. The union of these two is the development of the Germanic or modern world involving the political expression of the Christian principle. The first efforts of the union we find in the Middle Ages.[33] The Middle Ages are themselves an embodied contradiction. The contradiction is that the Christian principle which, if it be anything, must be a universal principle, losing itself in the whole of life in order to grow up, then, amid the conditions of human existence and association, attempted to realize itself

as a special institution as against all other institutions. The spiritual, instead of being the law of life, individual and political, was changed into a special kind of life, finding its own particular embodiment. Thus in the Middle Ages we have everywhere a dualism. On one side is the spiritual, on the other the secular and profane; on one side the church, on the other the empire. On one side the priest, on the other the laity. On one side theology, as a dogmatic body of absolute truth, on the other hand ordinary knowledge, the fluctuating mass of worthless opinion, and so indefinitely.

It was impossible, of course, that this contradiction could endure. The spiritual must either become nothing at all or it must become the animating principle of the entire temporal structure. The first realization of this fact constitutes what we call the Protestant Reformation. This took shape in the conception that the Christian principle, since universal, must be in direct relation with the heart and conscience of every man and hence that there is no need of an intermediate, special institution to preserve truth and the principle of salvation and to dole it out on harsh terms to the individual. This notion of the direct relation of divine truth to the individual as such is the heart of Luther's doctrine of justification by faith. Faith, then, is no mere intellectual conviction about certain theoretic formulae or about certain historic facts. It is simply the name for the capacity of the individual to have direct relations with the divine spirit. In Hegel's language,—it is the subjective and certain assurance of the eternal and essential truth of God. As such it is the organ by which the individual approaches God and therefore is substituted for the church as a middle term. "Hereby," says Hegel, "the new and final standard was raised about which the nations assembled. It is the banner of the free spirit, master of itself in the truth and only in the truth. This is the banner under which we serve and which we carry; this is the essential meaning of the reformation, namely; that the very nature of man defines him as free."[34] In other words, since man's spirit is in itself akin to the spirit of truth, man has of himself, without requiring any intervening authority, the power to get the truth, and living the light of this truth to be free.

145   The period since the Reformation has for its object the moulding of the world according to this Protestant principle. It has had to solve the problem of securing to the individual that actual access to truth which shall make him free. It was inevitable that this conception of individuality and truth should first be interpreted subjectively both in the individual and so far as society itself is concerned. In the individual it was seen in the formation of habits of minute introspective self-examination which gave to Protestant piety a pitiable and rational aspect of spiritual torment. The substitution of the individual for the church as the organ of truth at first woke the stream of capricious and introspective subjectivity. This conception of the individual as a source and test of truth also found expression in what is called the illumination, in the formal rationalism of the eighteenth century. The individual, conceiving that he had within himself the standard of truth, attempted to test all historical traditions and all political institutions by this private judgment of his own. Naturally, these objective institutions could not stand the test of formal reason and the result was that vast wave of skepticism regarding all religious truth expressed in theological form and regarding all social institutions which were so prevalent during the eighteenth century. This culminated in the French Revolution, which in principle was the conflict of the private reason of the individual with the public reason embodied in law, institution and tradition.

146   The consciousness by thought we have so far considered on its formal side, the attempt to measure objective institutions by the abstract reason of man. On the positive side man's consciousness of reason as incarnate in himself took the form, first, of science. Man became conscious of this presence of reason in himself and sought to work out its bearing through mastery of nature. Nature, which to earlier peoples had been either directly one with man or else a barrier to man, was seen to be so bound up with man's own life that he had to master its meaning in order to preserve his own mental integrity. So it came about as if God had for the first time just created the sun, moon, the stars, plants and animals, as though the laws of nature were for the first time settled. For men began first to have a real

interest in these things when they recognized their own reason in the reason pervading things. Second, thought was directed toward human action, toward the moral side of experience. A foundation was now sought for a law and morality, not in either the laws of nature nor in those of God's will externally made known, but as in man's own reason and will. Third, man became conscious that society and the State were themselves his own objective reason, they did not need to be overthrown in order that the individual might be free, but it was in and through them that the individual was free.

This realization of freedom of spirit which takes place in history constitutes the transition from objective to absolute spirit. In the theory of the subjective spirit we see the spirit as an activity working either upon or against or through a nature external to it. This externality is the limitation which makes the spirit subjective. In the objective spirit we find the spirit creating its own content, its own outward expression, first in the state, and then in the process of history. When we find that history itself marks the development of spirit we see that it is neither merely subjective nor merely objective, but that spirit itself is both the activity and the material of activity; that it is both form and content; that it is both the subject that undergoes development and the object through this development realized.

147

This brings us to the theory of the absolute spirit which Hegel treats under three heads: the philosophy of art, of religion and of philosophy itself. The conflict so far has been between the inner and the outer, between the meaning and the material which expresses this meaning, between idea and the form or object which conveys this idea, between the spiritual and the natural. In history we find rather the struggle onward toward the goal than the full fruition of the goal. Spirit is not yet one with itself but is still seeking this unity through the medium of the objective world.

148

Now, in art the sensuous and the ideal, the natural and the spiritual, are completely at one. In art, spirit finds spirit; it is reconciled with itself. Now this completeness of relation in which spirit constitutes both terms, in which spirit is both the feeling, knowing, acting subject, and the object of enjoyment and appreciation, is what Hegel

149

calls the absolute spirit. The work of art, in other words, has an infinite value. In art man is no longer struggling to express ideas in an alien material which resists his efforts, but is breathing out spiritual life through a medium as plastic and free as itself. In Hegel's language,—art is the representation of the absolute spirit in sensuous existence. In art the spirit exists and not simply strives to find existence. And again, in art, the spirit exists, the ideal or subjective side is not lost in the representation as it tends to be in the state and in history. The realization of the artistic idea occurs through three stages,—first, in symbolic art; second, in the classical; and thirdly, in romantic.

150   In symbolic art there is an attempt to convey the spirit by main strength, as it were, to embody[35] it forth physically. Historically, this stage of art is represented by gigantic pyramids, obelisks and huge grotesque statues of Oriental life. They really had not defined their own ideas. They had not mastered them and hence these ideas could not find expression in any clear outward form. They did not know what their own thoughts were, hence they could only hint at them, could only endeavor to make them real to themselves by some gigantic outward form.

151   In classical art, especially that of Greece, the idea was clearly and sharply defined and hence there was a perfect equation between the form and the content, that is, between the meaning of the work of art and the outward expression of it. This indeed is what we mean by classic art, the perfect interpenetration of soul and body. This art is plastic in the truest sense of the word; it alone truly deserves the name of art. Symbolic art is a little less than art; material still preponderates.

152   Romantic art, to which we now come, is a little more than art; in it the idea, the thought, becomes conscious of its full spiritual meaning, its own infinity. Hence it becomes impossible fully to express or convey the thought in outward forms. In romantic art there must be a phase of apparent incompleteness or inadequacy. The material is never able fully to convey the richness of the idea. Hence the romantic has to work by suggestion, by delicate hinting, by indicating more than is expressed. It does not tell the whole story like classic art, but

is aimed at the spectator; it hopes to rouse in his mind the emotions and ideas which were in the artist's mind but which were too great to be conveyed in any sensuous form. In other words, the spiritual element has become so thoroughly conscious of itself that it cannot get into an equilibrium with the sensuous element. It no longer expresses itself in the latter but rather uses it for its own end and aim. Forms of art repeat within their sphere the same principle of classification. Architecture is symbolic art; sculpture, classical art; painting and music, romantic.

Romantic art, since it expresses the predominance of the spiritual over the sensuous, marks the transition to religion. It may be said that art and religion both have the same content; both express and convey the same absolute truth. But art conveys this in the form of outer existences which are to be looked at and enjoyed by the individual. Religion conveys this truth with the individual's own inward experience in feeling and thought as its vehicle. As has been already said, the leading idea of absolute spirit is that spirit exists for and with itself. It is wholly one with itself, it is a system of the relations which constitute life. This principle must of course be revealed in religion also. Hence the development of religion is that of the religious consciousness, of consciousness which appreciates, at least in the form of feeling, that God is both the subject and object of life; that he is not unknowable nor far-away spirit, but is the spirit of all spirits. In other words, the development of religion is simply the progressive revelation of man to man, the revelation in which man discovers that the ground and aim of his existence is neither in man as a mere individual nor in a world of physical force external to him, but in a living process which unites within its activity him and all other persons, the process of nature itself. The development of religion, in other words, is man finding that the divine spirit is the source and end of all his activity and that therefore the absolute power of the universe is neither mere blind force nor simply an intelligent person outside of the world, that is, a living spirit who lives in and through the world.

Taken from this last standpoint it follows of course that this absolute spirit must reveal himself by the very law of his own being, that only in and through this self-revelation which constitutes his relation to nature and to finite spirits is he truly absolute spirit or God at all. Hence Hegel lays it down that the absolute spirit requires a finite spirit. Hegel treats of the historical development of religion under three heads: first natural religion, where man feels his unity with the power that is in the world but, in having realized this feeling, either makes objects of adoration or particular things in nature, thus identifying himself with them, or in some wild frenzy identifies himself with the absolute power of the world and thus claims the right to be and act as if he were this absolute power. In the second part Hegel treats the larger religions of the world, namely, the Jewish, which he regards as the religion of sublimity, the Greek, the religion of beauty and the Roman as the religion of external utility and aims and the conformity of means to ends. The third part treats of absolute religion which Hegel considers to be Christianity, treating Christianity neither simply as a historical event nor simply as a collection of dogmas, but rather as complete realization of the self-revelation of spirit. It is the main thought of the Christian religion that God is one with man and that there is a unity of the infinite and the finite and this truth, when grasped, not simply on the side of some outward event, not[36] of some supernatural dogma, is identical with the truth of philosophy itself. This constitutes the transition to the third part of the absolute spirit which Hegel calls philosophy.

Philosophy has exactly the same content as art and religion, excepting that which art took in the form of direct apprehension and religion took in the form of feeling and imagery, philosophy grasps as thought. This philosophy is not something by itself, Hegel says, as if before this time we had been going through the steps leading up to philosophy. Philosophy is nothing but a full realization of what has been thought and discussed previously. It is simply closing the work with which we have been previously occupied. It is getting that point of view whence we see nature, life and experience as elements in the active process of the self-revelation of spirit to spirit. It is the work of philosophy as such simply to place the dot which ends the sentence, thus for the first time getting the full meaning of that sentence.

Dewey's References in Hegel's Philosophy of Spirit (1897)

This bibliography is not in the original typescript; it has been addeed by the editors, based on references in the text. Bracketed notations regarding Dewey's library refer to copies of books in Dewey's personal and professional library, Special Collections Research Center, Morris Library, Southern Illinois University Carbondale.

Buckle, Henry Thomas. *History of Civilization in England*. 2 vols. New York: D. Appleton, 1876.

Caird, Edward. *Hegel*. Edinburgh and London: William Blackwood and Sons, 1883.

Draper, John William. *History of the Intellectual Development of Europe*. Rev. ed. 2 vols. New York: Harper and Brothers, 1876.

Hegel, Georg Wilhelm Friedrich. *Hegel's Philosophy of Mind*. Translated from the *Encyclopaedia of the Philosophical Sciences*, with five introductory essays, by William Wallace. Oxford: Clarendon Press, 1894.

———. *Lectures on the Philosophy of History*. Bohn's Philosophical Library. Translated from the 3rd German edition by John Sibree. London: George Bell and Sons, 1881.

———. *Lectures on the Philosophy of Religion*. Translated by E. B. Spiers and J. Burdon Sanderson. Vols. 2 and 3. London: Kegan Paul, Trench, Trübner, 1895.

———. *The Logic of Hegel*. Translated from the *Encyclopaedia of the Philosophical Sciences* by William Wallace. 2nd ed., rev. Oxford: Clarendon Press, 1892. [An annotated copy is in Dewey's library.]

———. *Philosophy of Right*. Translated by S. W. Dyde. London: George Bell and Sons, 1896.

Kant, Immanuel. *The Philosophy of Law: An Exposition of the Fundamental Principles of Jurisprudence as the Science of Right*. Translated by William Hastie. Edinburgh: T. and T. Clark, 1887.

Rosenkranz, Karl. *Georg Wilhelm Friedrich Hegel's Leben.* Berlin: Duncker and Humblot, 1844.

Royce, Josiah. "Two Philosophers of the Paradoxical." *Atlantic Monthly* 67 (January 1891): 45–60.

Tyndall, John. *Fragments of Science for Unscientific People: A Series of Detached Essays, Lectures, and Reviews.* New York: D. Appleton, 1871.

Wallace, William, trans. *Hegel's Philosophy of Mind.* Translated from the *Encyclopaedia of the Philosophical Sciences,* with five introductory essays. Oxford: Clarendon Press, 1894.

Dewey's References in Hegel's Philosophy of Spirit (1891)

In addition to the Caird, Hegel (*Lectures on the Philosophy of History*), and Royce citations above, Eliza Jane Read Sunderland listed several references in her notes for Dewey's 1891 Hegel's Philosophy of Spirit lectures. The abbreviations that Sunderland used are placed in square brackets.

Alexander, S. "Hegel's Conception of Nature." *Mind* 11 (October 1886): 495–523. [Mind Vol. IX or XI p. 495 article on Hegel's Conception of Nature by Alexander]

Harris, William Torrey. *Hegel's Logic.* Chicago: S. C. Griggs, 1890; 2nd ed., 1895. [Harris Hegel's Logic]

Hegel, Georg Wilhelm Friedrich. *The Introduction to Hegel's Philosophy of Fine Art.* Translated by Bernard Bosanquet. London: Kegan Paul, Trench, 1886. [Bosanquet Trans of Aesthetics]

———. *Introductory Lectures on Aesthetics.* Translated by Bernard Bosanquet. London: Kegan Paul, Trench, 1886. [Bosanquet Trans of Aesthetics]

Kedney, John Steinfort. *Hegel's Aesthetics.* Chicago: S. C. Griggs, 1885. [Kedney Hegel's Aesthetics]

Morris, George Sylvester. *Hegel's Philosophy of the State and of History.* Chicago: S. C. Griggs, 1887. [Morris Hegel's Phil of the State]

Seth Pringle-Pattison, Andrew. *The Development from Kant to Hegel.* London: Williams and Norgate, 1882. [Seth, From Kant to Hegel]

———. "Hegel: An Exposition and Criticism." *Mind* 6 (October 1881): 513–30. [Mind Vol. VI p. 513 article on Hegel by Seth]

Wallace, William. "Hegel." In *Encyclopaedia Britannica,* 9th ed., 11:612–21. New York: Samuel L. Hall, 1878. [Enc. Brit. Article Hegel]

Notes

All quotations of Dewey's writings are from *The Collected Works of John Dewey, 1882–1953*, 37 vols., edited by Jo Ann Boydston (Carbondale: Southern Illinois University Press, 1969–1990). The volumes were published as *The Early Works: 1881–1898* (*EW*), *The Middle Works, 1899–1924* (*MW*), and *The Later Works, 1925–1953* (*LW*).

PREFACE

1. *Annual Register*, July 1896–July 1897 with announcements for 1897–98 (Chicago: University of Chicago Press, 1897). According to the register, Dewey offered the course in the autumn, winter, and spring quarters. The course is also listed in the 1897/1898 register. Although Dewey read Hegel in the German editions then available, the English translations of Hegel from that period should be mentioned. William Wallace's translation of Hegel's "Lesser Logic" was first published in 1873; its second edition was released in 1892. Wallace's translation of Hegel's *Philosophy of Mind* was published in 1894. Hegel's *Aesthetics* or *Philosophy of Fine Art* was available only in partial translation at this time. William Bryant, one of the St. Louis Hegelians, published a translation of part 2 in 1879: Hegel, *The Philosophy of Art: Being the Second Part of Hegel's Æsthetik, in which Are Unfolded Historically the Three Great Fundamental Phases of the Art-Activity of the World*, trans. W. M. Bryant (New York: D. Appleton, 1879). Another partial translation appeared in the Griggs Philosophical Classics series edited by G. S. Morris and Dewey: John Steinfort Kedney, *Hegel's Aesthetics: A Critical Exposition* (Chicago: S. C. Griggs, 1885). The first third of Kedney's book was a translation of the beginning of part 1. Kedney's translation was followed by two more partial translations in 1886: Hegel, *The Philosophy of Art: An Introduction to the Scientific Study of Aesthetics*, ed. Karl Ludwig Michelet, trans. William H. Hastie (Edinburgh: Oliver and Boyd, 1886), and Bernard

Bosanquet, *The Introduction to Hegel's Philosophy of Fine Art* (London: Kegan Paul, Trench, 1886). The *Phenomenology* was not translated in its entirety until 1910: Hegel, *The Phenomenology of Mind*, trans. J. B. Baillie (London: Swan Sonnenschein, 1910). A partial translation of Hegel's philosophy of law was published in 1873: James Hutchison Sterling, *Lectures on the Philosophy of Law: Together with Whewell and Hegel, and Hegel and Mr. W. R. Smith, a Vindication in the Physico-Mathematical Regard* (London: Longmans, Green, 1873).

DEWEY'S NATURALIZED PHILOSOPHY OF SPIRIT AND RELIGION
John R. Shook

1. Many scholarly debates over whether Dewey's pragmatism broke sharply with Hegelian idealism are recounted in John R. Shook, *Dewey's Empirical Theory of Knowledge and Reality* (Nashville: Vanderbilt University Press, 2000). My confidence in the strong continuity thesis increased after reading James A. Good, *A Search for Unity in Diversity: The "Permanent Hegelian Deposit" in the Philosophy of John Dewey* (Lanham, Md.: Lexington Books, 2005). Our inquiries into Dewey's formative years are indebted to Steven Rockefeller, *John Dewey: Religious Faith and Democratic Humanism* (New York: Columbia University Press, 1991).

2. Rockefeller describes Dewey's later reflections on his youthful religious views in *John Dewey*, 37–38.

3. For an overview of the New Divinity movement's final phase see Allen C. Guelzo, *Edwards on the Will: A Century of Theological Debate in America* (Middletown, Conn.: Wesleyan University Press, 1989), 272–78.

4. Joseph Ratner investigated the intellectual influences on Dewey in Burlington, and his findings have been essential for subsequent biographers. In a letter to Francis C. Becker, Ratner reports that "the Pastor Brastow was quite an extraordinary intellectual, his sermons were courses of lectures and Dewey was unquestionably deeply attracted to and by him. Brastow left B. for a professorship in Yale Divinity in 1884. From 1873 to 1882 Brastow stirred up a hornet's nest of theological-orthodoxy controversy—Brastow was trying to liberalize the doctrine and succeeded within ten years in so successfully beating down Yale that the latter invited him as prof. These years are Dewey's growing up years and he breathed the stuff in without any effort. The Vt. univ. professors—nearly to a man congr. ministers—were in the liberal-orthodox brawl officially and semi-officially; Dewey's phil. prof—Torrey—was a member of Dewey's church and very active in it at that time and till his death." *The Correspondence of John Dewey*, vol. 3: *1940–1953*, ed.

Larry A. Hickman (Charlottesville, Va.: Intelex Corporation, 2005), #07171, 7 December 1946.

5. See Rockefeller, *John Dewey*, 40–43.

6. Lewis Orsmond Brastow, "The Religious Factor in Education," *New Englander and Yale Review* 43 (January 1884): 23.

7. Dewey's adoption of the Edwardean theory of personal responsibility is examined in John R. Shook, "Jonathan Edwards' Contribution to John Dewey's Theory of Moral Responsibility," *History of Philosophy Quarterly* 21 (July 2004): 299–312.

8. This account is related in *Dialogue on John Dewey*, ed. Corliss Lamont (New York: Horizon, 1959), 15–16. See also Rockefeller, *John Dewey*, 56–64.

9. James Marsh, "Editor's Introduction" (1839), reprinted in *Aids to Reflection*, in *The Collected Works of Samuel Taylor Coleridge* (Princeton, N.J.: Princeton University Press, 1993), 9:491–529. On Coleridge and free will, see Mary Anne Perkins, *Coleridge's Philosophy* (Oxford: Oxford University Press, 1994), 189–204. On Coleridge and philosophy of religion, see Douglas Hedley, *Coleridge, Philosophy and Religion: Aids to Reflection and the Mirror of the Spirit* (Cambridge, UK: Cambridge University Press, 2000).

10. See Rockefeller, *John Dewey*, 48–49.

11. Max Eastman, "John Dewey," *Atlantic Monthly* 168 (December 1941): 673

12. George S. Morris, *Philosophy and Christianity* (New York: Robert Carter and Brothers, 1883). See also R. M. Wenley, *The Life and Work of George Sylvester Morris* (New York: Macmillan, 1917).

13. *EW* 2:290–91.

14. Dewey's gradual development of his pragmatism from idealistic principles is examined in detail by Shook, *Dewey's Empirical Theory of Knowledge and Reality*, chaps. 2–5.

15. *EW* 2:7.

16. Dewey, *The Study of Ethics* (1894), *EW* 4:259. Some Dewey scholars have mistaken Dewey's rejection of Green's approach to the moral life as a sign that Dewey was departing from idealism entirely. However, Dewey's worries over Green's excessively rationalistic theory of morality were inevitable, since Dewey understood himself as defending the worthy aspects of the more organic Hegelian idealism.

17. A key writing in addition to *The Study of Ethics* during this period is "Moral Theory and Practice" (1891), *EW* 3:93–109. See Shook, *Dewey's Empirical Theory of Knowledge and Reality*, chaps. 3 and 4.

18. See especially Dewey, "Christianity and Democracy" (1893), *EW* 4:3–10, and "Reconstruction" (1894), *EW* 4:96–105.
19. Dewey, "Naturalism" (1902), *MW* 2:142.
20. Dewey, "Beliefs and Existences" (1906), *MW* 3:98.
21. Dewey, "Review of George Santayana, *The Life of Reason, or The Phases of Human Progress*" (1906), *MW* 3:323.
22. Dewey, "Humanism and Naturalism" (1912), *MW* 7:213–17.
23. Dewey, "Freedom of Will" (1911), *MW* 6:465–66.
24. Dewey, *Human Nature and Conduct* (1922), *MW* 14:9.
25. No large-scale study of Dewey's fulfillment of Hegel's theory of freedom has been published. Studies of Hegel most useful for revealing the broad common ground between Dewey and Hegel on rights and freedom include Alan Patten, *Hegel's Idea of Freedom* (Oxford: Oxford University Press, 2002); Frederick Neuhauser, *Foundations of Hegel's Social Theory: Actualizing Freedom* (Cambridge, Mass.: Harvard University Press, 2000); and Steven B. Smith, *Hegel's Critique of Liberalism: Rights in Context* (Chicago: University of Chicago Press, 1989). Chapter 5 of Good's *A Search for Unity in Diversity* yields more needed clues about the Dewey–Hegel stance toward freedom and rights.
26. See Shook, "Dewey's Vision of Equal Opportunity for Education in a Democracy," in *Pragmatism and the Problems of Race*, ed. Bill Lawson and Donald Koch (Bloomington: Indiana University Press, 2004), 48–72.
27. Dewey, "Religion and Our Schools" (1908), *MW* 4:176.
28. *MW* 14:181.
29. *LW* 1:314.
30. *LW* 4:244.
31. *LW* 9:18.
32. *LW* 9:15–16.
33. *The Correspondence of John Dewey*, vol. 3: *1940–1953*, ed. Larry A. Hickman (Charlottesville, Va.: Intelex Corporation, 2005), #08049, 14 January 1935.
34. Dewey, "A God or The God?" (1933), *LW* 9:218.
35. Dewey constructs this dilemma for liberal theology in his review of *Is There a God? A Conversation*, by Henry Nelson Wieman, Douglas Clyde Macintosh, and Max Carl Otto (Chicago: Willett, Clark, 1932), *LW* 9:213–22.
36. *LW* 9:29.
37. Ibid.
38. *LW* 9:35.
39. Ibid.

40. *LW* 9:36.
41. *LW* 9:57.
42. Dewey, "Dr. Dewey Replies" (1933), *LW* 9:224 (italics in original).
43. *LW* 4:242.
44. *LW* 4:243.
45. *LW* 9:11.
46. *LW* 9:16, 19. The complicated task of distilling Dewey's conception of the religious experience from his numerous but confusing explications has occupied many Dewey scholars. Besides those already cited, another should be recommended: Milton R. Konvitz, Introduction to *The Quest for Certainty*, *LW* 9:xi–xxxii.
47. *LW* 5:71–72.
48. *LW* 5:72. Hegel makes this point in several places, most notably in *Philosophy of Right*, §153.
49. *MW* 4:175.
50. *EW* 4:3.
51. *EW* 4:9.
52. *EW* 4:5. Hegel made similar claims about Jesus in "The Spirit of Christianity and Its Fate," in *Hegel's Early Theological Writings*, trans. T. M. Knox (Chicago: University of Chicago Press, 1948), esp. 212–25. See also "The Life of Jesus" and "The Positivity of the Christian Religion," both in that same volume.
53. Dewey, "Creative Democracy—The Task Before Us" (1939), *LW* 14:226–27.
54. *EW* 2:292–93.
55. *EW* 3:321–22.
56. Dewey, "Intelligence and Morals" (1908), *MW* 4:39.
57. Dewey, "Individuality, Equality, and Superiority" (1922), *MW* 13:297.
58. Dewey, *Ethics* (1932), *LW* 7:350.
59. Dewey, "What I Believe" (1930), *LW* 5:273–74.
60. Dewey, *A Common Faith* (1934), *LW* 9:55–56.
61. Ibid., *LW* 9:57–58.

REREADING DEWEY'S "PERMANENT HEGELIAN DEPOSIT"
James A. Good

1. Dewey, *Experience and Nature* (1925), *LW* 1:13, 28.
2. Ibid., 1:14.
3. Ibid., 1:6.
4. Hegel, *Phenomenology of Spirit*, trans. A. V. Miller (Oxford: Oxford University Press, 1977), §39.

5. My own understanding of Hegel is indebted to what is known as "the nonmetaphysical reading" of his philosophy. For an introduction to that reading, see H. Tristram Engelhardt and Terry Pinkard, eds., *Hegel Reconsidered: Beyond Metaphysics and the Authoritarian State* (Boston: Kluwer, 1994).

6. This clarifies Tom Rockmore's claim that "Hegel . . . proposes a new paradigm of systematic knowledge without foundations, with an obvious, but as yet largely unexplored relation to pragmatism." Tom Rockmore, *On Hegel's Epistemology and Contemporary Philosophy* (Atlantic Highlands, N.J.: Humanities Press International, 1996), 90.

7. Dewey, *Psychology* (1887), *EW* 2:291.

8. Dewey, "The Psychological Standpoint" (1886), *EW*, 1:123–43; "Psychology as Philosophic Method" (1886), *EW* 1:144–67; and "Illusory Psychology" (1887), *EW* 1:168–75.

9. Dewey, "The Psychological Standpoint," *EW* 1:122–43. For Dewey's first use of the term "psychological standpoint," see John Dewey to H. A. P. Torrey, 17 November 1883. Shook provides further insight into the "the psychological standpoint" by discussing its use in the mid-1880s. John R. Shook, *Dewey's Empirical Theory of Knowledge and Reality* (Nashville: Vanderbilt University Press, 2000), 44–46.

10. Dewey, "The Psychological Standpoint," *EW* 1:124.

11. Hegel, *Phenomenology of Spirit*, §802. It is worth noting that Robert Solomon detected a similarity between Hegel's conception of experience to that found in the "practical-minded writings of the American pragmatists William James and John Dewey." Solomon, *In the Spirit of Hegel: A Study of G. W. F. Hegel's* Phenomenology of Spirit (New York: Oxford University Press, 1983), 11.

12. Klaus Hartmann, "Hegel: A Non-Metaphysical View," in *Hegel: A Collection of Critical Essays*, ed. A. MacIntyre (Garden City, N.Y.: Doubleday, 1972), 101–24.

13. Hegel, *Hegel's Science of Logic*, trans. A. V. Miller (Atlantic Highlands, N.J.: Humanities Press, 1969), 63.

14. Dewey, "The Postulate of Immediate Empiricism," *MW* 3:158–67.

15. Dewey, "The Need for a Recovery of Philosophy," *MW* 10:46.

16. Hegel to Schelling, 2 November 1800. Quoted in Steven B. Smith, *Hegel's Critique of Liberalism: Rights in Context* (Chicago: University of Chicago Press, 1989), 56.

17. John Dewey to Alice Dewey, 10 October 1894.

18. For a prime example, see chapter 4 of Dewey, *Democracy and Education*, *MW* 9:46–58.

19. Dewey, *Human Nature and Conduct,* MW 14:196.

20. Because of the richness of the German term *Geist,* which is translated as "spirit" in A.V. Miller's translation of the *Phenomenology of Spirit,* and as "mind" in William Wallace's translation of the *Philosophy of Mind,* I use "spirit" and "mind" interchangeably throughout this chapter, as does Dewey in his lecture.

21. Josiah Royce, "Two Philosophers of the Paradoxical," *Atlantic Monthly* 67 (1891): "Hegel," 45–60; "Schopenhauer," 161–73. With an additional introduction on modern philosophy, and some minor changes, both essays appear in Josiah Royce, *The Spirit of Modern Philosophy* (New York: W. W. Norton, 1892). Royce notes that he was influenced by Rudolf Haym's and James Hutchison Stirling's "estimates of Hegel's personality," which is apparent in his negative comments, but he also drew on Karl Rosenkranz's biography (see Royce, *Spirit of Modern Philosophy,* 194). Karl Rosenkranz, *Georg Wilhelm Friedrich Hegel's Leben* (Berlin: Duncker and Humblot, 1844).

22. Dewey had been familiar with Rosenkranz since the early 1880s. After submitting two articles to William Torrey Harris for publication in the *Journal of Speculative Philosophy,* "The Metaphysical Assumptions of Materialism" and "The Pantheism of Spinoza," Dewey offered to translate Rosenkranz's introduction to "Kirchmann's ed. of Hegel's Encyclopädie," which, he stated, he had "been reading recently." Dewey to W. T. Harris, 1 July 1882; and Dewey to W. T. Harris, 22 October 1881. Rosenkranz wrote two introductions to Hegel's *Encyklopädie der philosophischen Wissenschaften im grundrisse,* an 1845 edition published in Berlin by Duncker and Humblot, and an 1870 edition published in Berlin by L. Heimann. Although Jay Martin states that Dewey's translation of Rosenkranz's introduction appeared in the July 1882 issue of the *Journal of Speculative Philosophy,* it was never published. Martin, *The Education of John Dewey* (New York: Columbia University Press, 2002), 57. In fact, Harris had already published Thomas Davidson's translation of the introduction in the *Journal of Speculative Philosophy.* Karl Rosenkranz, "Introduction to Hegel's *Encyclopedia of the Philosophical Sciences,*" trans. Thomas Davidson, *Journal of Speculative Philosophy* 5, no. 3 (July 1871): 234–50.

23. Karl Löwith, *From Hegel to Nietzsche: The Revolution in Nineteenth-Century Thought,* trans. David E. Green (New York: Columbia University Press, 1964), 53–59; and John Toews, *Hegelianism: The Path toward Dialectical Humanism, 1805–1841* (New York: Cambridge University Press, 1980), 71–154, 203–42.

24. One hundred twenty-nine pages in the *Journal of Speculative Philosophy* were devoted to translations of Rosenkranz's writings. On the importance of Rosenkranz's Center Hegelianism and its influence on American

Hegelianism see Michael H. DeArmey and James A. Good, eds., *Origins, the Dialectic, and the Critique of Materialism*, vol. 1 of *The St. Louis Hegelians* (Bristol, Eng.: Thoemmes Press, 2001), xvii–xviii.

25. The literature on the modern problematic is voluminous. I have found two sources particularly relevant here, however. See Smith's discussion of "the divided self" in *Hegel's Critique of Liberalism*, 17–31; and Richard Bernstein's discussion of "the Cartesian Anxiety" in *Beyond Objectivism and Relativism: Science, Hermeneutics, and Praxis* (Philadelphia: University of Pennsylvania Press, 1988), 16–20. Elsewhere, I have argued that Smith's interpretation of Hegel sheds important light on the way Dewey read Hegel by the mid-1890s. James A. Good, *A Search for Unity in Diversity: The "Permanent Hegelian Deposit" in the Philosophy of John Dewey* (Lanham, Md.: Lexington Books, 2006).

26. Karl Rosenkranz, "Hegel as Publicist," trans. G. Stanley Hall, *Journal of Speculative Philosophy* 6 (1872): 258–79.

27. The most important biographical studies of the late twentieth century and early twenty-first century are H. S. Harris, *Hegel's Development: Toward the Sunlight, 1770–1801* (Oxford: Clarendon Press, 1972); John Toews, *Hegelianism* (Cambridge: Cambridge University Press, 1980); H. S. Harris, *Hegel's Development: Night Thoughts (Jena, 1801–1806)* (Oxford: Clarendon Press, 1983); Laurence Dickey, *Hegel: Religion, Economics, and the Politics of Spirit, 1770–1807* (Cambridge: Cambridge University Press, 1983); Terry Pinkard, *Hegel: A Biography* (Cambridge: Cambridge University Press, 2000); and Horst Althaus, *Hegel: An Intellectual Biography*, trans. Michael Tarsh (Cambridge: Polity Press, 2000). All of these biographers have benefited from Wilhelm Dilthey's rediscovery of Hegel's early theological writings, which were initially published by Hermann Nohl in 1907. Hegel, *Hegels theologische Jugendschriften*, ed. Nohl (Tübingen: Mohr/Siebeck, 1907). T. M. Knox translated these essays as *Hegel's Early Theological Writings* (Chicago: University of Chicago Press, 1948). These biographers also benefited from the study of Hegel's "minor" political writings, which were translated in 1964 by T. M. Knox. Hegel, *Hegel's Political Writings*, trans. T. M. Knox, with an introductory essay by Z. A. Pelczynsky (Oxford: Clarendon Press, 1964). According to Frederick G. Weiss, Pelczynsky's introductory essay "quietly embarrassed" the myth of "Hegel's reactionary conservatism . . . into silence." Weiss, "A Critical Survey of Hegel Scholarship in English: 1962–1969," 27. Three more of Hegel's early essays have been translated as Hegel, *Three Essays, 1793–95: The Tübingen Essay, Berne Fragments, The Life of Jesus*, ed. and trans. Peter Fuss and John Dobbins (Notre Dame, Ind.: University of Notre Dame Press, 1984).

28. Cf. Dewey's claim that "the very meaning and purport of [his] empirical method is that things are to be studied on their own account, so as to find out what is revealed when they are experienced." Dewey, *Experience and Nature* (1925), LW 1:14.

29. All further references to Dewey's lecture "Hegel's Philosophy of Spirit," part 2 of this volume, will be given by page number within parentheses.

30. Dewey made similar statements about Hegel in 1891: "When Hegel calls thought objective he means just what he says: that there is no special, apart faculty of thought belonging to and operated by a mind existing separate from the outer world. What Hegel means by objective thought is the meaning, the significance of the fact itself; and by methods of thought he understands simply the processes in which this meaning of fact is evolved. . . . [Hegel's] contention is not that thought, in the scholastic sense, has ontological validity, but that in fact, reality is significant." Dewey, "The Present Position of Logical Theory" (1891), *EW* 3:136–37, 139.

31. Cf. Dewey's assertion that, for Hegel, "All so-called faculties of mind are simply stages in this development of knowledge" (¶87).

32. Dewey, "The Reflex Arc Concept in Psychology" (1896), *EW* 5:105.

33. For James's use of what he calls "the psychologist's fallacy," see William James, *The Principles of Psychology* (New York: Dover Publications, 1950), 1:196. Shook, *Dewey's Empirical Theory of Knowledge and Reality*, 49. On this point Shook takes issue with J. E. Tiles's claims about James's influence on Dewey. Cf. Tiles, *Dewey* (London: Routledge, 1988), 29.

34. Shook, *Dewey's Empirical Theory of Knowledge and Reality*, 49.

35. At this time, Peirce actually had little influence on Dewey. For Peirce's take on the differences in their approaches to logic, see Charles S. Peirce, *Collected Papers*, ed. Charles Hartshorne and Paul Weiss (Cambridge: Harvard University Press, 1958), 8:180–84, 189.

36. Dewey must have drawn on Rosenkranz for his knowledge of Hegel's early theological writings. His perception of those essays as primarily concerned with sociopolitical issues is not unusual. Though he overstates his case, Walter Kaufmann has called these essays Hegel's "anti-theological writings," which reveals how they might undermine the neo-Hegelian's theological reading of Hegel. Kaufmann, "Hegel's Early Anti-Theological Phase," *Philosophical Review* 63, no. 1 (1954): 3–18. Harris's reading of these essays, in *Hegel's Development: Toward the Sunlight*, provides an important contrast to Kaufmann's.

37. Louis Menand, *The Metaphysical Club: A Story of Ideas in America* (New York: Farrar, Straus and Giroux, 2001), 265.

38. Hegel, *Elements of the Philosophy of Right*, ed. Allen Wood, trans. H. B. Nisbet (Cambridge: Cambridge University Press, 1991), 20.

39. See Allen Wood's introduction to Hegel, *Elements of the Philosophy of Right*, vii–xxxii; T. M. Knox, "Hegel and Prussianism," in *Hegel's Political Philosophy*, ed. Walter Kaufmann (New York: Atherton Press, 1970), 21–22; Kenneth Westphal, "The Basic Context and Structure of Hegel's *Philosophy of Right*, in *The Cambridge Companion to Hegel*, ed. Frederick Beiser (Cambridge: Cambridge University Press, 1993), 234–44; and Shlomo Avineri, *Hegel's Theory of the Modern State* (Cambridge: Cambridge University Press, 1972), chaps. 6–9.

40. Hegel, *The Logic of Hegel, Translated from* The Encyclopaedia of the Philosophical Sciences, 3rd ed., trans. William Wallace (Oxford: Oxford University Press, 1975), §6. ("The Lesser Logic" is a popular name for Hegel's Encyclopedia logic.)

41. Ibid., §94. Cf. Hegel's claim in the *Science of Logic* that "what is actual can act." Hegel, *Hegel's Science of Logic*, 546.

42. Cf. Kenneth R. Westphal, *Hegel's Epistemological Realism: A Study of the Aim and Method of Hegel's* Phenomenology of Spirit (Dordrecht: Kluwer Academic, 1989).

43. Although Dewey does not mention it, it is useful to bear in mind that Hegel's reflections on religion took place as Robespierre disastrously sought to impose his Festival of the Supreme Being on the French people in 1794.

44. This passage is reminiscent of Dewey's description of the influence of Thomas Huxley on him as an undergraduate: "It is difficult to speak with exactitude about what happened to me intellectually so many years ago, but I have an impression that there was derived from that study a sense of interdependence and interrelated unity that gave form to intellectual stirrings that had been previously inchoate, and created a kind of type or model of a view of things to which material in any field ought to conform. Subconsciously, at least, I was led to desire a world and a life that would have the same properties as had the human organism in the picture of it derived from study of Huxley's treatment." Dewey, "From Absolutism to Experimentalism" (1930), *LW* 5:148.

45. Dewey, *A Common Faith* (1934), *LW* 9:41.

46. I elaborate on Dewey's debt to Hegel on this particular issue in James A. Good, "Beyond 'Sushiology': John Dewey on Diversity," *Pluralist* 1, no. 2 (2006): 123–32.

47. Despite popular characterizations of Hegel as a monist, in the *Phenomenology* he lampoons Schelling's identity philosophy, claiming it tries

"to palm off its Absolute as the night in which . . . all cows are black—this is cognition naively reduced to vacuity." In a subsequent passage, Hegel described monism as "a monochromatic formalism." The problem, Hegel avers, is that monisms deny the reality of the "self-originating, self-differentiating wealth of shapes" that we encounter in experience. Hegel, *Phenomenology of Spirit*, §§15, 16.

48. Dewey, "Self-Realization as the Moral Ideal" (1893), *EW* 4:52, 53; Dewey, "Green's Theory of the Moral Motive" (1892), *EW* 3:160.

49. Dewey, "The Metaphysical Method in Ethics" (1896), *EW* 5:25, n. 3. See also Dewey, "Beliefs and Existences" (1906), *MW* 3:86, n. 3.

50. It is important to understand that by "infinity" Hegel does not mean a mathematical concept. In point of fact, he refers to an infinite progression as a "bad infinity." Infinity, for Hegel, is a completed whole, something that is not dependent on anything else; much like Anaximander's concept of *apeiron*, it is that which is unbounded. Michael Inwood, *A Hegel Dictionary* (Oxford: Blackwell Publishers, 1992), 139–42.

51. In this passage, Dewey is essentially paraphrasing Hegel: "If soul and body are absolutely opposed to one another . . . then there is no possibility of any community between them. . . . Therefore, the question arose as to how the contradiction, to wit, that entities which are absolutely independent and for themselves, are yet in unity with one another, could be solved. The question as thus posed was unanswerable. But it is just this form of the question that must be recognized as inadmissible; for in truth the immaterial is not related to the material as a particular is to a particular, but as the true universal which overarches and embraces particularity is related to the particular; the particular material thing in its isolation has no truth, no independence in face of the immaterial. Consequently, the standpoint which separates them is not to be regarded as final, as absolutely true. On the contrary, the separation of the material and the immaterial can be explained only on the basis of the original unity of both." Hegel, *Philosophy of Mind*, 33.

52. Cf. Hegel, *The Logic of Hegel*, §153.

53. Hegel, *Hegel's Science of Logic*, 559.

54. Similarly, Dewey writes, "Means and ends are two names for the same reality. The terms denote not a division in reality but a distinction in judgment." Dewey, *Human Nature and Conduct* (1922), *MW* 14:28, cf. 160.

55. Hegel, *The Logic of Hegel*, §153.

56. Hegel, *Hegel's Science of Logic*, 559.

57. Dewey, "The Metaphysical Assumptions of Materialism" (1882), *EW* 1:3–9.

58. By my count, Hegel devotes about 28 of the 315 pages in Wallace's edition of the *Philosophy of Mind* to the philosophy of history, about 9 percent. By contrast, Dewey discusses Hegel's philosophy of history for at least 14 pages, depending on how one counts it, out of 81, about 17 percent.

59. Hegel, *Philosophy of Mind,* §484.

60. See Hegel's formulation of this point: "A history without such aim and such criticism would be only an imbecile mental divagation, not as good as a fairy tale, for even children expect a motif in their stories, a purpose at least dimly surmisable with which events and actions are put in relation." Hegel, *Philosophy of Mind, Translated from* The Encyclopaedia of the Philosophical Sciences, trans. William Wallace and A.V. Miller (Oxford: Clarendon Press, 1971), §549.

61. Although his conclusions may be different, methodologically, I believe Dewey's own writings on the history of philosophy are essentially Hegelian, even in works in which he criticizes Hegel. See, for example, Dewey, *German Philosophy and Politics* (1915), *MW* 8:135–204; Dewey, *Reconstruction in Philosophy* (1920), *MW* 12:77–202; and Dewey, *The Quest for Certainty* (1929), *LW* 4:1–255.

62. Frederick Beiser, "Introduction to the Bison Edition," in Hegel, *Lectures on the History of Philosophy* (Lincoln: University of Nebraska Press, 1995), 1:xiii.

63. Dewey, "Time and Individuality" (1940), *LW* 14:110, 113.

64. Dewey, *Experience and Nature* (1925), *LW* 1:91–92.

65. Dewey, *Art as Experience* (1934), *LW* 10:30–31.

66. Dewey, *Knowing and the Known* (1949), *LW* 16:125.

67. See Dewey to William James, 6 May 1891. "Would it horrify you, if I stated that your theory of emotions (where you seem to me to have completely made out your case) is good Hegelianism? Although, of course, Hegel gets at it in a very different way. But according to Hegel a man can't feel his own feelings unless they go around, as it were, through his body." See also Dewey, "The Theory of Emotion" (1894–95), *EW* 4:171. "In my *Psychology,* e.g., p. 19 and pp. 246–49 [*EW* 2:21–22, 215–17], it is laid down, quite schematically, that feeling is the internalizing of activity or will. There is nothing novel in the doctrine; in a way it goes back to Plato and Aristotle. But what first fixed my especial attention, I believe, upon James's doctrine of emotion was that it furnishes this old idealistic conception of feeling, hitherto blank and unmediated, with a medium of translation into the terms of concrete phenomena. I mention this bit of personal history simply as an offset to

those writers who have found Mr. James's conception so tainted with materialism. On the historical side, it may be worth noting that a crude anticipation of James's theory is found in Hegel's *Philosophie des Geistes*, §401."

68. On Hegel's expressivism see Charles Taylor, *Hegel* (Cambridge: Cambridge University Press, 1975).

69. Hegel, *Phenomenology of Spirit*, §20.

70. Hegel, *Hegel's Science of Logic*, 633. Hegel, *Phenomenology of Spirit*, §§20, 39ff.

71. See Hegel, *The Logic of Hegel*, §43.

72. As Dewey rather awkwardly attempted to explain this to James, "the unity of Hegel's self (& what Caird is driving at) is not a unity in the stream as such, but of the *function* of this stream, the unity of the world (content) which it bears or reports—It may seem strange to call this unity Self, but while Kant undoubtedly tried to make *an* agent out of this (and Green follows him) [*sic*] But Hegel's agent (or Self) is simply the universe doing business on its own account. . . . But Hegel seems to me intensely modern in his spirit, whatever his garb, and I don't like to see him dressed up as Scholasticus Redivivus—although of course his friends, the professed Hegelians, are mainly responsible for that." Dewey to William James, 6 May 1891. In this letter, it is apparent, once more, that Dewey distinguished Hegel from the British neo-Hegelians.

73. Hegel, *Philosophy of Mind*, §432.

74. Hegel, *Philosophy of Right*, §41.

75. Dewey, *Ethics* (1932), *LW* 7:275.

76. For a more complete development of this point about Hegel's conception of freedom, see Alan Patten, *Hegel's Idea of Freedom* (New York: Oxford University Press, 1999), 53–73.

77. Here Dewey appears to draw on Hegel, *Philosophy of Right*, §§202–5.

78. See Dewey's 1908 comment on Hegel: "The outcome was the assertion that history is reason, and reason is history: the actual is rational, the rational is the actual. It gave the pleasant appearance (which Hegel did not strenuously discourage) of being specifically an idealization of the Prussian nation, and incidentally a systematized apologetic for the universe at large. But in intellectual and practical effect, it lifted the idea of process above that of fixed origins and fixed ends, and presented the social and moral order, as well as the intellectual, as a scene of becoming, and it located reason somewhere within the struggles of life." Dewey, "Intelligence and Morals" (1908), *MW* 4:43.

79. Dewey is certainly not alone in this judgment. Many scholars argue that Hegel does not demonstrate that his particular conceptions of the monarchy, the legislature, and the civil service bureaucracy are truly necessary for the state to play the role he envisions for it, which is the actualization of freedom. See Patten, *Hegel's Idea of Freedom*, 166.

80. Hegel, *Philosophy of Right*, §§258, 267–68.

HEGEL'S PHILOSOPHY OF SPIRIT: 1897, UNIVERSITY OF CHICAGO
John Dewey

Dewey gave this seminar, "Hegel's Philosophy of Spirit," in 1897 at the University of Chicago. The *University of Chicago Annual Register* for July 1896–July 1897, listing courses for 1897–1898, described the "Seminar in the Philosophy of Hegel," courses 45, 46, 47, as follows (169):

> Hegel's lesser Logic and Philosophy of Mind, as translated by Wallace, will be made the basis of study. Points of connection with the thought of his predecessors, especially Kant and Spinoza, will be studied, and Hegel's own ideas will be further developed by reference to selected portions of the Phenomenology, the Philosophy of Law, and the Aesthetics. For graduate students.
>
> Autumn, Winter, and Spring Quarters, '97–8; Mondays, 4:00–6:00 P.M.
>
> Head Professor Dewey

The same announcement was made in the 1894–1895 *Annual Register*, listing courses for 1895–1896 (with the notation "Not to be given in '95–6"), the 1895–1896 *Annual Register*, listing courses for 1896–1897 (with the notation "Not to be given in '96–7"), and, for the last time, in the 1897–1898 *Annual Register*, listing courses for 1898–99.

A mimeographed typescript for Hegel's Philosophy of Spirit class lecture notes, 103 pages (originally part of the H. Heath Bawden Collection) is located in the Joseph Ratner/John Dewey Papers, Box 49, folder 7, Special Collections Research Center, Morris Library, Southern Illinois University Carbondale. On the cover sheet is written "H. Heath Bawden Vassar College Poughkeepsie." The notetaker is unknown.

Corrections made in pencil in the typescript are discussed in the notes.

A similar set of class lecture notes for Dewey's 1891 Hegel lectures, handwritten by Eliza Jane Read Sunderland (Sunderland Manuscript Collection, Bentley Historical Library, University of Michigan), indicates that Dewey had worked out his Hegel lectures by 1891. The *Calendar of the University of*

Michigan for 1891–92 and for 1892–93 lists Dewey as teaching "Hegel's Logic, Wallace's translation."

Three numbered footnotes, apparently added to the typescript after 1897, have been treated as editorial notes and are cited below in notes 26, 27, and 28.

1. Eliza Jane Read Sunderland also cited this Josiah Royce article in her lecture notes for Dewey's 1891 Hegel's Philosophy of Spirit lectures (Sunderland Manuscript Collection, Bentley Historical Library, University of Michigan). The reference list for these lectures includes additional references cited by Sunderland.

2. "Whereupon I thought out the following principle, a rather painful one for me, but still a very profound one, namely, that in youth . . . one can't eat as much as one wants, while in age one doesn't want to eat as much as one can" (Royce, "Two Philosophers of the Paradoxical," 50).

3. Edward Caird, *Hegel*, 12.

4. In the original typescript "latter" is written above "former," which is crossed out.

5. "To the Greek, the idea of the fatherland, his State" (Caird, *Hegel*, 31).

6. The phrase "laboured and which formed his persistent motive" is also from Caird (ibid.).

7. Dewey used the phrase "the solvent word" in "Nature and Its Good: A Conversation," in *Middle Works* 4:26: "But when Arthur was speaking, I felt that perhaps this disagreement exists precisely because the solvent word had not been uttered." William Torrey Harris (in the preface to *Journal of Speculative Philosophy* 1 (1867): 1) also used "the solvent word," one that changes or adapts to conditions or circumstances.

8. In the original typescript "made" is altered from "may be" by hand.

9. Dewey is apparently referring to Immanuel Kant's *The Philosophy of Law*.

10. In 1802 Hegel and Friedrich Wilhelm Joseph von Schelling founded, cowrote, and coedited the short-lived *Critical Journal of Philosophy* in Jena. Their introduction to the journal was published in 1801.

11. Hegel's *The Phenomenology of Mind* was not translated in its entirety until 1910 (trans. J. B. Baillie, published in London by Swan Sonnenschein).

12. Instead of "blackness of night" the original typescript reads "blankness of night."

13. In the original typescript "conformable" is altered by hand from "comfortable."

14. In the original typescript "as" is written above "on," which is crossed out.
15. In the original typescript "into" is altered by hand from "in."
16. In the original typescript "universals" is written above "particulars," which is crossed out.
17. Instead of "cannot avoid" the typescript reads "can avoid."
18. In the original typescript "do not" is inserted by hand.
19. In the original typescript "but on" is inserted by hand.
20. Instead of "genus" the original typescript reads "genius."
21. Instead of "Thus the soul" the original typescript reads "This the soul."
22. In the original typescript "yet" is written above "and," which is crossed out.
23. In the original typescript "the" is written above "each," which is crossed out.
24. In the original typescript the phrase "themselves out of their intelligence" is bracketed by hand and "omit" is written above it.
25. The noun that one expects after "mutual" is missing in the original typescript.
26. Here a footnote was apparently added later to the typescript, citing John Watson, "The New 'Ethical' Philosophy," *International Journal of Ethics* 9 (July 1899): 413–34.
27. A partially illegible note apparently added later to the typescript reads: "Known by peripherally excited new aesthetics ss [sic] chiefly."
28. A note apparently added later to the typescript reads: "The civil society of Arabs is simply an extended family idea."
29. Instead of "stating" the original typescript reads "starting."
30. Instead of "morality was directly" the original typescript reads "morality direct."
31. Instead of "and yet as" the original typescript reads "and yet."
32. Instead of "was in this" the original typescript reads "was this."
33. Instead of "in the Middle Ages" the original typescript reads "in the modern ages."
34. Caird, *Hegel*, 22.
35. In the original typescript "embody" appears as "body" with extra space before it.
36. Instead of "not of some" the original typescript reads "but of some."

Index

absolute
  and experience, 50, 59, 127–28
  as God, 12, 58, 66, 84, 89, 110, 161, 167
  and knowledge, 58, 120, 132
  as mind, 73–74
  as process, 57–58, 72, 84, 114
  spirit, 19, 60, 74, 84–85, 88–89, 110, 117–19, 147–48, 171–72
Addams, Jane, 28
anthropology, 74, 120–23
Aquinas, Thomas, 7
Aristotle, 60, 188
art, 88–89, 120, 127, 142, 164, 171–73
atheism, 5–6, 19, 29, 31, 36–37, 40–43
  and agnosticism, 41

Beiser, Frederick, 78, 186, 188
belief
  practical, 4–5, 21–22
  religious, 6, 11, 17–18, 44, 104, 168
Berkeley, George, 96
Brastow, Lewis Ormand, 6, 7, 8, 15
Buckle, Henry Thomas, 76, 77, 78, 123, 175

Caird, Edward, 62
Calvin, John, 7
Calvinism, 6–10
Cartesianism, 20, 63, 74
Christianity, 7, 17, 66, 89, 98–99, 174
  democratic, 14, 19–20, 31, 45, 59
  individualistic, 84, 114, 147, 167–69
  liberal, 30, 47–48
  New Divinity, 6

  pluralistic, 46–47
  social gospel, 17
civil society, 87, 108, 156–58
Civil War, U.S., 8
Coleridge, Samuel Taylor, 10, 15, 96
Comte, Auguste, 77
conscience, 48, 104–5, 153–55, 164, 169
consciousness, 18, 79–83, 102–3, 108, 119–23, 131–33
  self-consciousness, 59–60, 77, 88, 115–16, 134–39, 160–65
  See also mind
contract, 85, 149
  social, 46

democracy
  faith in, 19–20, 26, 31–32, 41–43, 50–55, 109
  and government, 87–89
  and morality, 7–9, 29–30, 52–55
  participatory, 26–27, 50–52, 160
  and religion, 47–51
Dewey, Alice, 3, 61, 182
Dewey, John
  atheism, 35–41
  early religion, 6–11
  Hegelianism, 12–17, 58–61
  political theory, 47–55
  pragmatism, 23–26
  social theory, 26–30
Dewey, Lucinda, 6
dogma, 46, 49, 58, 69, 106–7, 168–69, 174
Draper, John William, 76, 77, 78, 123, 175

{ 193 }

INDEX

Eastman, Max, 11
Edwards, Jonathan, 6, 7, 15
Emerson, Ralph Waldo, 93
Emmons, Nathaniel, 6
empiricism, 14, 83
　immediate, 59
England, 46, 125
Enlightenment, 44, 69, 73, 99, 105, 112
ethics, 8, 86–87, 151, 164–65
　religious, 31–32, 71, 99
　social, 28–29, 31, 51–52, 155–57

faith
　democratic, 19–20, 26, 31–32, 41–43, 50–55, 109
　moral, 13–14, 34–36, 36–37, 53–55
　religious, 4–5, 11, 14–16, 30–31, 34–37, 53–54, 99–101, 167, 169–70
family, 84, 87, 108, 147, 156–57
fatalism, 33–35
Fichte, J. G., 67, 69, 70, 71, 72, 99, 103, 106, 109, 110, 112
freedom
　and democracy, 8, 27, 86–88, 113, 148
　and individuality, 9, 55, 73, 84–85, 88, 105–6, 109
　and morality, 23–25
　of religion, 48
　and spirit, 55, 77–78, 88, 117–19, 137–38, 146–47, 161–62, 171
French Revolution, 65

Germany, 93
God
　as absolute, 12, 58, 66, 84, 89, 110, 147, 161, 167, 173
　and humanity, 10, 12, 14, 17, 37–40, 49–50, 89, 97–101, 114, 162, 167, 174
　and morality, 5–6, 9, 13–14, 17, 31–32, 36–42, 48, 71, 99
Good, James A., 19, 178, 180, 184, 186
government
　and freedom, 48, 50, 73, 157
　function of, 26–29, 46, 87–88, 157–60
　social contract, 46
　and war, 28
　See also state

Greece, 99, 151, 163, 165, 172
Green, Thomas Hill, 15, 16, 71, 72

Habermas, Jürgen, 44
habit, 80–81, 130–31
Haym, Rudolf, 62
Hegel, G. W. F.
　and absolute, 50, 56–59, 61, 72, 74, 117–20, 171–74, 186, 187
　and aesthetics, 89, 171–73
　on causation, 75–80, 85, 115
　on history, 76–79, 88, 105, 123–24, 147, 151, 153, 159–74, 188, 188, 188
　influence on Dewey, 5–6, 12–15, 17, 19, 28–29, 31, 44, 47, 55, 58–59, 61–89, 178, 179, 180, 184, 186
　on morality, 85–87
　and philosophical method, 16, 58, 63–72, 94–96, 103–7, 111, 128, 185, 187
　and philosophical psychology, 59–60, 64–65, 79–84, 96, 108, 112, 114–48, 154–55, 185, 188
　and political philosophy, 14, 27–29, 48, 62–63, 67, 73, 84–88, 97–101, 104–5, 112–13, 124, 137, 148–53, 155–60, 180, 186, 186, 190
　on religion, 5–6, 12, 14, 50, 68, 89, 97–101, 174, 186
　and spirit, 50, 55, 56, 59–61, 72–74, 84, 88–89, 102–4, 107, 111–20, 123, 126, 138–39, 161–65, 171–74
history, 76–77, 119
　philosophy of, 76, 78, 159
　and spirit, 59–60, 73, 84, 88, 160–65, 171–72
Hobbes, Thomas, 7
Hölderlin, Friedrich, 65, 96
humanism, 19, 41, 74
　and ideals, 28, 34, 41
　religious, 20, 31, 54
　secular, 19
Hume, David, 96
Huxley, Thomas Henry, 11

idealism
　absolute, 19, 59
　German, 11–12, 16–17

organic, 14, 19–20, 40
romantic, 10
subjective, 64, 71
imagination, 37, 86, 141–44
intelligence, 10, 23–24, 83–84, 120–21, 142–44
   democratic, 51–52
   social, 14–15, 20, 26

James, William, 4, 29, 44, 65
Jesuits, 101
Journal of Speculative Philosophy, 62–63

Kant, Immanuel,
   and ethics, 85–86
   and idealism, 10, 12, 16, 57–58, 133–40
   and religion, 67, 69, 99–100
   and transcendentalism, 58, 81–82, 105–9
Klopstock, F. G., 96
knowledge
   and inquiry, 5, 14–16, 21–23, 41, 44, 58, 65
   and mind, 10, 14–15, 64, 95, 131–33, 140–45
   as representational, 20, 63–64, 74, 95
   self-knowledge, 88–89, 114, 139

law
   consciousness of, 133–34
   natural law, 81, 171
   and right, 29, 73, 84, 125, 147–51
   and state, 100–1, 119–20, 159–60, 164–66
   and will, 86, 98, 102, 113, 153–56
Locke, John, 27

Marsh, James, 10
matter, 19
   and soul, 74, 76, 122
   and spirit, 15, 123
memory, 140–45
Menand, Louis, 66
Middle Ages, 168–69
Mill, John Stuart, 52–53, 54
mind
   absolute, 61–62, 73–74, 84, 88

and knowledge, 10, 14–15, 64, 95, 131–33, 140–45
and nature, 14, 112, 115–19, 123
and speech, 80–81, 129–30, 143
See also consciousness
morality, 5
   and ideals, 9–10, 28, 34, 41
   and religion, 31–32, 71, 99
Morris, George Sylvester, 12

natural piety, 30–35, 42
naturalism, 5–6, 18–19, 42–43
nature
   and science, 18, 22–23, 170
   and spirit, 10, 14, 103, 107, 112, 115–19, 122–23, 163–65, 171

Otto, Max Carl, 36

panentheism, 38
pantheism, 12, 16, 38, 122
particular, 70, 115, 118, 128, 131, 153
   and universal, 86–87, 102, 121, 126, 142–43, 150, 154–55
Peirce, Charles S., 22, 65
perception, 83–84, 111–12, 115, 133–34, 140–44
   and sensation, 84, 115, 127–30, 139–40, 157
phenomenology, 59, 81, 120, 131
piety, 13, 19–20, 30–35, 43, 99, 170
Plato, 7, 10, 108, 188
Pond, Enoch, 6
pragmatism, 4–5
   and community, 48–49
   and knowledge, 14–16, 21–23, 31–32
Protestant, Protestantism, 10, 15, 44, 47–48, 93, 104
Protestant Reformation, 46, 169–70
psychology, 4, 14, 59, 114–15, 120, 138
   functional, 21, 64–65
   social, 15, 20, 24, 82–83
punishment, 85, 98, 149–50, 155
Pythagoreans, 94

Quakers, 101

rationalism, 99, 170
  and empiricism, 21–22
Rawls, John, 44
reason
  and experience, 21, 84, 133–34, 139–44
  and knowledge, 5, 14–15, 21–23, 44, 68, 65, 75, 83, 113–14, 138–39
  and state, 159–60, 170
  and spirit, 10, 19, 58, 67–68, 83, 100, 120–21, 133, 138, 146, 170–71
  and understanding, 65, 75, 146
  and will, 16, 83, 121, 150–51
religion, 7, 17, 66, 89, 98–99, 174
  and democracy, 47–51
  and ethics, 5, 13–14, 31–32, 36–42, 48, 71, 99
  and faith, 4–5, 14–16, 30–1, 34–37, 53–54, 99–101, 167, 169–70
  and God, 37–40, 97–101, 161–62, 173–74
  and humanism, 20, 31, 54
  and science, 4–5, 21, 44
  and spirit, 12–14, 20, 34, 43, 84, 97, 104, 110–11, 167–69, 173–74
  and state, 45, 46, 65, 68–69, 97–101, 104
religious experience, 4
religious spirit, 12–14, 20, 34, 43, 84, 97, 104, 110–11, 167–69, 173–74
responsibility
  intelligent, 5, 16
  moral, 7–9, 15, 23–24, 44, 55
right
  civil, 4, 27–28
  and freedom, 27–29, 54, 84–86, 153–56
  and law, 29, 73, 84, 125, 147–51, 166
  natural, 48
Romanticism, 10, 33–34, 89, 96, 153, 172–73
Rosenkranz, Karl, 62, 63, 94, 176, 183, 184, 185
Rousseau, Jean-Jacques, 71, 108
Royce, Josiah, 62, 94, 176, 183, 191, 194

Santayana, George, 19, 35
Schelling, F. W. J., 69, 70, 71, 96, 110, 111, 112

Schiller, Johann, 96
science
  and democracy, 26–27
  and history, 78, 162
  method, 22–23
  and naturalism, 18, 170
  and religion, 4–5, 21, 44
self-
  consciousness, 59–60, 77, 88, 115–16, 134–39, 160–65
  realization, 12–13, 15, 24, 38
Shook, John R., 56, 65, 178, 179, 180, 182, 185
sin, 69, 98, 102, 104
Socrates, 151
Sophists, 151
soul, 8–9, 76
  and body, 80–81, 123–24, 128–29, 139, 172
  and spirit, 74, 77, 114–15, 120–22, 125–32
speech, 80–81, 129–30, 143
Spinoza, Baruch, 33, 43, 183, 190
spirit
  absolute, 19, 50, 57–61, 72–4, 84–85, 88–89, 110, 117–19, 147–48, 171–72
  and art, 88–89, 142, 171–73
  and consciousness, 79–83, 134–39, 160–65
  and freedom, 55, 77–78, 88, 117–19, 137–38, 146–47, 161–62, 171
  in history, 59–60, 73, 84, 88, 160–65, 171–72
  and individuality, 55, 77, 84, 88, 113–14, 132, 163–65
  and nature, 10, 14, 103, 107, 112, 115–19, 122–23, 163–65, 171
  objective, 13–15, 19, 28–29, 50, 55, 60–61, 66, 71–73, 107–10, 116, 124, 143–44, 147, 157–59, 171
  and psychology, 14–15, 59, 64–65, 82–83, 114–15, 120, 138
  and reason, 10, 19, 67–68, 83, 100, 120–21, 133, 138, 146, 170–71
  and state, 28, 50, 55, 73, 84, 99, 101–4, 124, 147, 156–61, 164–65, 170

religious, 12–14, 20, 34, 43, 84, 97, 104, 110–11, 167–69, 173–74
subjective, 60, 77, 113–14, 116, 119–21, 132, 138, 147–50, 171
universal, 68, 71, 77, 82–83, 102–3, 109–10, 112, 121–23, 134, 137–38, 149–50
St. Louis Hegelians, 62
state
  and freedom, 48, 50, 73, 113, 119, 157–59, 166–8, 171–72
  function of, 26–29, 67, 87–88, 157–60
  and religion, 45, 46, 65, 68–69, 97–101, 104
  and rights, 27
  and spirit, 73, 84, 147, 156–61, 164–65
  and war, 28
  See also government
Sunderland, Eliza, 176, 190, 191

Torrey, H. A. P., 10
tragedy, 34–36
transcendentalism, 19, 21, 63, 93

truth, 21–22, 81
  and conscience, 155
  and democracy, 49, 170–71
  and faith, 169
  and thought, 30, 32, 96, 106–7, 132–33
Tufts, James H., 28
Tyndall, John, 122

understanding, 65, 75, 146
universal
  and particular, 86–87, 102, 121, 126–28, 142–43, 146, 150, 154–56
  spirit, 68, 71, 77, 82–83, 102–3, 109–10, 112, 121–23, 134, 137–38, 149–50
universalism, 7–8, 12, 20, 24

war, 28
Whitman, Walt, 11
will, 8, 77, 83, 86, 148–49
  free will, 146
  and law, 86, 98, 102, 113, 153–56
  and reason, 121, 150–51
Wordsworth, William, 11, 96

AMERICAN PHILOSOPHY
Douglas R. Anderson and Jude Jones, series editors

Kenneth Laine Ketner, ed., *Peirce and Contemporary Thought: Philosophical Inquiries.*

Max H. Fisch, ed., *Classic American Philosophers: Peirce, James, Royce, Santayana, Dewey, Whitehead, second edition.* Introduction by Nathan Houser.

John E. Smith, *Experience and God, second edition.*

Vincent G. Potter, *Peirce's Philosophical Perspectives.* Ed. by Vincent Colapietro.

Richard E. Hart and Douglas R. Anderson, eds., *Philosophy in Experience: American Philosophy in Transition.*

Vincent G. Potter, *Charles S. Peirce: On Norms and Ideals, second edition.* Introduction by Stanley M. Harrison.

Vincent M. Colapietro, ed., *Reason, Experience, and God: John E. Smith in Dialogue.* Introduction by Merold Westphal.

Robert J. O'Connell, S.J., *William James on the Courage to Believe, second edition.*

Elizabeth M. Kraus, *The Metaphysics of Experience: A Companion to Whitehead's "Process and Reality," second edition.* Introduction by Robert C. Neville.

Kenneth Westphal, ed., *Pragmatism, Reason, and Norms: A Realistic Assessment—Essays in Critical Appreciation of Frederick L. Will.*

Beth J. Singer, *Pragmatism, Rights, and Democracy.*

Eugene Fontinell, *Self, God, and Immorality: A Jamesian Investigation.*

Roger Ward, *Conversion in American Philosophy: Exploring the Practice of Transformation*.

Michael Epperson, *Quantum Mechanics and the Philosophy of Alfred North Whitehead*.

Kory Sorrell, *Representative Practices: Peirce, Pragmatism, and Feminist Epistemology*.

Naoko Saito, *The Gleam of Light: Moral Perfectionism and Education in Dewey and Emerson*.

Josiah Royce, *The Basic Writings of Josiah Royce*.

Douglas R. Anderson, *Philosophy Americana: Making Philosophy at Home in American Culture*.

James Campbell and Richard E. Hart, eds., *Experience as Philosophy: On the World of John J. McDermott*.

John J. McDermott, *The Drama of Possibility: Experience as Philosophy of Culture*. Edited by Douglas R. Anderson.

Larry A. Hickman, *Pragmatism as Post-Postmodernism: Lessons from John Dewey*.

Larry A. Hickman, Stefan Neubert, and Kersten Reich, eds., *John Dewey Between Pragmatism and Constructivism*.

Dwayne A. Tunstall, *Yes, But Not Quite: Encountering Josiah Royce's Ethico-Religious Insight*.

Josiah Royce, *Race Questions, Provincialism, and Other American Problems, Expanded Edition*. Edited by Scott L. Pratt and Shannon Sullivan.

Lara Trout, *The Politics of Survival: Peirce, Affectivity, and Social Criticism*.

www.ingramcontent.com/pod-product-compliance
Lightning Source LLC
Chambersburg PA
CBHW031245290426
44109CB00012B/442